DATE DUE

NO 17 '98			
MR 15 '99			
MR 29 '99			
DE 9			
JE 2 0 '12			

DEMCO 38-296

Understanding
Pride and Prejudice

The Greenwood Press "Literature in Context" Series

Understanding *To Kill a Mockingbird*: A Student Casebook to Issues, Sources, and Historical Documents
Claudia Durst Johnson

Understanding *The Scarlet Letter*: A Student Casebook to Issues, Sources, and Historical Documents
Claudia Durst Johnson

Understanding *Adventures of Huckleberry Finn*: A Student Casebook to Issues, Sources, and Historical Documents
Claudia Durst Johnson

Understanding *Macbeth*: A Student Casebook to Issues, Sources, and Historical Documents
Faith Nostbakken

Understanding *Of Mice and Men, The Red Pony,* and *The Pearl*: A Student Casebook to Issues, Sources, and Historical Documents
Claudia Durst Johnson

Understanding Anne Frank's *The Diary of a Young Girl*: A Student Casebook to Issues, Sources, and Historical Documents
Hedda Rosner Kopf

UNDERSTANDING

Pride and Prejudice

A STUDENT CASEBOOK TO ISSUES, SOURCES, AND HISTORICAL DOCUMENTS

Debra Teachman

The Greenwood Press
"Literature in Context" Series
Claudia Durst Johnson, Series Editor

GREENWOOD PRESS
Westport, Connecticut • London

Library of Congress Cataloging-in-Publication Data

Teachman, Debra, 1955–
    Understanding Pride and prejudice : a student casebook to issues,
sources, and historical documents / Debra Teachman.
        p.   cm.—(The Greenwood Press "Literature in context" series,
ISSN 1074–598X)
    Includes bibliographical references and index.
    ISBN 0–313–30126–3 (alk. paper)
    1. Austen, Jane, 1775–1817. Pride and prejudice. 2. Literature
and society—England—History—19th century. I. Title.
II. Series.
PR4034.P72T43   1997
823'.7—dc21   97–5858

British Library Cataloguing in Publication Data is available.

Library of Congress Catalog Card Number: 97–5858
ISBN: 0–313–30126–3
ISSN: 1074–598X

First published in 1997

Greenwood Press, 88 Post Road West, Westport, CT 06881
An imprint of Greenwood Publishing Group, Inc.

Printed in the United States of America

The paper used in this book complies with the
Permanent Paper Standard issued by the National
Information Standards Organization (Z39.48–1984).

10 9 8 7 6 5 4 3 2 1

Contents

Acknowledgments

I could not have undertaken and completed this book without the support of many good friends and colleagues. I thank them for their help.

I thank my colleague in the English Department at Marshall University, Lee Erickson, who suggested that my teaching and writing talents might join together well in this project. His generosity of spirit and faith in my abilities led him to recommend me to the series editor, Claudia Durst Johnson, who would have been unlikely to come across my name in any other way.

I thank Claudia Durst Johnson for taking a chance on a first-time author and for being a constant source of assistance and positive reinforcement.

I thank Barbara A. Rader, executive editor at Greenwood Publishing, for leading me patiently and supportively through the writing process.

For assistance with research I am particularly grateful to David Gray, interlibrary loan librarian at Marshall University. Without his help and that of his staff, many of the eighteenth- and nineteenth-century sources included here would have been much more difficult to access.

I thank my colleague and friend, Josephine Bloomfield, assistant professor of English at Ohio University, for her generosity in providing me with a place to stay and access to the Ohio University library collection during portions of my research. The collection at Ohio University yielded some of the most important source material for this book.

I thank the Graduate School at Marshall University for the research grant that enabled me to take a summer off from teaching in order to devote myself fully to researching and writing this book.

Finally, to Wayne Jones, I am grateful for your support always. No matter how difficult or joyful the situation, you share it with me. Thank you.

Introduction

At the end of the eighteenth century and beginning of the nine-teenth, England was confronting many ideas and situations that were new and threatening to the status quo. Revolution was in the air. In 1775 the American colonies had revolted against English control and subsequently, by means of war, broke entirely from England, disposing even of the idea of monarchy by establishing a republican form of government. In the 1780s the French overthrew their monarchy, executing many members of the royal family and the aristocracy in their revolt against the tyranny of class designated by birth. Both revolutions were driven by powerful forces—the pursuit of equality for all men (though limited by race and/or prop-erty ownership) and the idea that individuality and merit count for more than birthright and inheritance.

In addition to the revolutions of France and the United States, there were other, not so well received, responses to the ideas of equality and individuality among men. Women of the better edu-cated classes began to imagine a world in which they could have the same rights and privileges as men. Mary Wollstonecraft's land-mark work of early feminism, *A Vindication of the Rights of Woman* (1792), was written after she had published a much less famous work, *A Vindication of the Rights of Men* (1790), in which she defended individuality and equality among men against attacks by conservatives like the English philosopher Edmund Burke. Theories of equality and individuality were not only stretched to include women, however; they were also expanded as arguments against slavery based on race, leading to a strong movement for the abolition of slavery in England in the early nineteenth century.

Into this whirl of revolutionary zeal and the English government's repressive reactions came the novels of Jane Austen. In the first two decades of the nineteenth century, during which all of Austen's novels were published, the British government passed repressive measures that severely limited what could be published without danger of the author and the publisher or printer being accused and convicted of sedition. As a result of those measures, the publishing industry increasingly turned to "safe" topics—like that of "3 or 4 Families in a Country Village," as Jane Austen once called the subject of her novels. Her books do not make explicit statements about the political issues confronting England, but they do illustrate much of English life in those difficult times. Austen, by focusing on the activities of only a few country families, deflects attention from the overtly political, while in fact showing how social class, patronage, and privilege affected the average English person, male and female. Her novels, therefore, are enacted against the background of both physical revolution and a major revolution of thought, but they do not directly express any particular argument.

One result of Austen's refusal (or perhaps inability, given the prevailing political climate in the publishing world) to engage directly in the argument over revolutionary ideas has been that readers have often been able to find support for diverse views in Austen's works. Some literary and social critics have labeled her conservative, antifeminist, and supportive of the status quo; others have described her novels as subversive, and claimed that they support individualism, set out for ridicule the traditionally accepted views of the aristocratic, patriarchal structure of British society, and encourage change to a more egalitarian society with equity of treatment under the law for all people, including women, servants, and children. Both sides of this argument can find support in the novels, as can many less extreme positions.

The fact that Austen's novels can be interpreted in a wide variety of ways does not, however, make them wishy-washy or politically passionless. Instead, it demonstrates their complexity, the complexity of human nature. Just as we find ourselves interpreting the events of our own lives and those of the people we know from our own political, social, and personal perspectives, so too do we interpret the lives of Austen's characters from our individual perspectives. Unlike many others of her period, Austen has not written didactic tracts that inform us of the "proper" way to think about issues of class, gender, marriage, and social structure; instead she shows us the reality of life, from her own perspective, for men and women in the small towns and country villages of England. She shows us human nature in many forms and many situations, enabling us to make judgments about the society in which her characters live.

Because Austen focuses on human nature instead of on politics, her works transcend time and place. As readers of the late twentieth century, we are able to relate to the experiences of her characters, to put ourselves in their places, and to try to determine what we or those we know would do in similar situations. Thus, her novels remain fresh, providing not only an enjoyable read but an opportunity to examine human nature in a different historical setting.

Pride and Prejudice, perhaps more than any other novel of its time, places us clearly within the context of English society at the time of such revolutionary struggles. It shows us the effects of those struggles on members of the English gentry and lower aristocracy who have no direct connection to the revolutions under way. On the surface, it is a love story, but under the surface, it is informed by many facets of society of which late twentieth-century readers tend to have little understanding. Knowing this, I have provided information about Austen's time and place from a variety of sources, including literary, historical, legal, sociological, and religious works. Throughout the following chapters, documents from these diverse perspectives illuminate different aspects of Austen's fiction.

The first chapter is a literary analysis of *Pride and Prejudice*. It focuses on the central issue of the novel, marriage, and how various characters relate to the societal situation that makes marriage such a dominant focus of the lives of women in Austen's time. Issues of class, property, and gender pervade the novel, as does the conflict between the way things "are done" (the status quo) and individualism. Austen takes great care with even the most minor of her characters, drawing portraits that encourage her readers to examine the relationships of each character to the others in careful detail.

Chapter 2 discusses in some depth the law and custom of Austen's time as they applied to marriage and inheritance. With so much of the plot hinging on inheritance laws that are, by our standards, antiquated and illogical, some grasp of these laws is essential to a thorough understanding of the novel. It is equally necessary to understand the laws involving marriage. Whereas marriage as an institution was much the same in Austen's time as in our own, the legal consequences for both parties (and for the families involved) were far-reaching, because divorce was almost unknown, and because women relinquished many rights when they married.

Chapter 3 discusses marriage from the viewpoint of other eighteenth-century English writers. The obligations and expectations of each spouse differed widely from those of the present day, and it is instructive to examine the attitudes of Austen's contemporaries on the institution of marriage.

Chapter 4 examines in some detail the role of the unmarried woman. *Pride and Prejudice* is, in one sense, a novel about how important it was for women of Austen's time to marry—and to marry well. To comprehend the importance of marriage, one must understand what the alternative meant for women of the late eighteenth century. The excerpts from William Hayley's essay on old maids vividly illustrate the prejudices to which unmarried women were subject. Jane West and Mary Wollstonecraft describe some of the difficulties unmarried women faced because few economic and social opportunities were available to them in English society. Other sources describe the situation of unmarried women who did not lead a life of chastity, and that of widows, who in English society generally had greater power and social standing than their never-married counterparts.

Chapter 5 looks at educational opportunities and expectations for the young woman of the gentry or aristocracy, including what could be expected when one was sent away to a girls' boarding school and what one might expect to learn if kept at home and tutored by a mother or a governess. There were no legal requirements in Austen's time that girls receive any formal education whatsoever, and modern readers are often puzzled to find that embroidery, drawing, singing, and dancing were highly regarded as educational pursuits.

Chapter 6 examines twentieth-century parallels to issues in *Pride and Prejudice*. The details have changed, but in many cases the issues themselves remain the same. This chapter focuses on how courtship and marriage customs both resemble and differ from those of Austen's time. It shows that finding and maintaining personal partnerships (whether in marriage or in less legally formalized situations) remains one of the dominant issues of our society today, and how educational opportunities and the ability to lead a fulfilling life as a single woman have increased dramatically since Austen's time.

Excerpts from and references to a wide variety of documents are included in these chapters, all of them chosen to expand one's understanding of the novel. They include the following:

- a literary study
- commentaries on eighteenth-century English law
- eighteenth-century literary essays
- eighteenth-century advice manuals
- eighteenth-century educational treatises
- historical reports
- a newspaper article
- magazine articles

Each issue explored as well as the supporting documents is introduced by an essay explaining its significance in relation to *Pride and Prejudice*. Also included are Topics for Written or Oral Exploration and Suggested Readings.

Page numbers in parentheses following quoted material refer to the texts listed in the Suggested Readings at the end of each chapter. Original spellings have been used in most cases; some have been modified, however, in the interests of clarity. Quotations from *Pride and Prejudice* are from the J. M. Dent and Sons edition published in London in 1906.

Understanding
Pride and Prejudice

Pride and Prejudice

Mr Darcy requested to be allowed the honor of her hand

Figure 1.1. Illustration of Darcy requesting Elizabeth's hand, from a nineteenth-century edition of *Pride and Prejudice. Source: The Novels of Jane Austen: Pride and Prejudice.* Boston: Little, Brown, 1892, frontispiece.

1 ———————————

Literary Analysis: *Pride and Prejudice*

"It is a truth universally acknowledged, that a single man in possession of a good fortune, must be in want of a wife." With that line, claimed by some scholars to be the most famous opening line of all fiction, Jane Austen begins *Pride and Prejudice*. That one line introduces several of the major issues and themes that have been explored in the novel throughout the past two centuries: marriage, wealth, class, property, propriety, and a debate over the existence of universal truth. Moreover, these are not merely issues of historical significance; they retain their relevance as we move into the twenty-first century, still trying to determine how best to deal with issues of love, money (or the lack of it), and proper behavior in a world that resists simple solutions to complicated issues.

Pride and Prejudice has often been depicted as a simple story of love between a wealthy, proud aristocrat and an intelligent, beautiful young woman born into a family of five sisters with little financial security. Elizabeth, the second of five daughters in the Bennet family, is bright, attractive, witty, and of good moral character. Her father is a gentleman, a term used in Austen's time to denote a man who has sufficient income from property he owns not to have to work in a profession or trade to support his family. He has inherited a small estate that supplies enough money to provide for his family during his lifetime; however, since he has no son, the estate will pass, after his death, to his cousin, Mr. Collins. As a result, his wife and daughters will not have sufficient income to support themselves comfortably after Mr. Bennet dies. This fact leads Mrs. Bennet to focus all of her attention on getting husbands for her daughters so that they will be provided for later in life. The interrelated issues of financial security and marriage are, therefore, at the heart of the novel.

Elizabeth meets Mr. Fitzwilliam Darcy at a party in the neighborhood. They begin their acquaintance by insulting one another, develop strong feelings for each other, and eventually recognize those feelings as love. Obstacles to their marrying include differences in wealth and social position, the behavior of members of their respective families, and their own proud and prejudiced views of themselves and each other, which temporarily prevent them from communicating openly and honestly with each other about their feelings, hopes, dreams, and fears. Ultimately, as in all of Jane Austen's novels, the right people marry one another, having learned lessons about themselves and the world around them as they endure and overcome the difficulties set in their paths by themselves and others.

This summary of the plot is accurate, as far as it goes, but it does the novel great disservice to oversimplify the plot and the issues dealt with in such a way. In fact, *Pride and Prejudice* explores the moral and social conditions of life in the early nineteenth century in ways that enable us both to understand that earlier time better and to examine with greater insight our own attitudes and actions within the moral and social conditions of life in our own time, enabling us to determine ways in which our decisions about love, marriage, and proper behavior reflect our own truths about what is ultimately right and wrong. Yet, for all of its emphasis on morality, the novel is not preachy. Through her ironic style, Austen causes us to laugh at and with her characters as we explore our own pridefulness and prejudices along with theirs.

EARLY NINETEENTH-CENTURY ENGLAND

Jane Austen set *Pride and Prejudice* in the time in which she lived, the first decades of the nineteenth century, generally known as the Regency period in England. In order to understand the world of the novel, one must understand something of the society it represents. This society was highly stratified: aristocrats tended to socialize with other aristocrats; the gentry (generally considered to be upper middle class by today's standards) socialized with other gentry; tradespeople socialized with tradespeople, the working poor with the working poor, and the poverty-stricken with other nonworking poor. Yet, while this stratification was firmly in place, it was not absolute. Tradespeople who earned sufficient money might buy their way into the gentry or, within a few generations, even into the aristocracy (examples in *Pride and Prejudice* include Sir William Lucas, a tradesman who bought a country estate and retired to become a gentleman, and Mr. Bingley, whose father earned his fortune in trade). Those born into the gentry might either rise in stature through economic and social good fortune or fall into straitened circumstances by loss of money, property, or good name. Thus, the class system in England at the beginning of the nineteenth century, though rigid in theory, in fact had considerable room for mobility.

Social position, however, tended to be established in terms of families, not individuals. A woman, for example, generally held the social position of her father, to be replaced by that of her husband if she married. Her children were considered to have the social rank of their father, unless they attached themselves to other family members who ranked higher socially. Thus, the Bingley family, whose wealth came from successful trade in earlier generations, were, by virtue of that wealth, raised to the level of gentry—upper gentry, in fact, as is evident by their ability to rent Netherfield Park. Although the bulk of the money belongs to Mr. Bingley, the social status of his unmarried sister is high because she has attached herself to his household. Likewise, any scandal committed by one member of a family implicated all—and could literally destroy the chances of the unmarried women in the family to find respectable mates. Thus, Lydia Bennet's running off with Mr. Wickham presents a danger not only to her own reputation and her own future but to those of her sisters as well.

Men were somewhat less reliant on family respectability than women, but the social status of their families mattered to them also. A man born into an aristocratic or upper gentry family could generally count on having a strong start in life. If he were the eldest son (as is Mr. Darcy), he would inherit the bulk of his family's estate (property and money). If he were a younger son, his family's influence and financial support would generally provide him with either a lesser estate or with training for a profession (generally the church, the law, or the military) together with money or influence enough to obtain a professional position once his training was complete.

Women born into aristocratic or gentry-level families had many fewer choices than their brothers. They generally inherited very little money and property (relative to their older brothers), and no professions were open to them in which they could make respectable names for themselves. If a woman from the gentry did not marry and had no family members who could take her in and provide for her, often the only somewhat respectable alternative was to become a governess or a teacher in a school for girls. Even those positions, however, lowered her social status, making it almost impossible for her to attract a husband who could provide for her adequately. To make matters worse, the income she could earn through such means was, in most cases, barely enough for survival. Thus marriage to an economically respectable man was considered to be the only legitimate choice for most women of the gentry or the aristocracy.

Jane Austen herself never married, despite having at least two suitors. She lived with her mother and her sister Cassandra for her entire adult life. The three of them had to rely on Austen's brothers to supplement the small income they had inherited from Austen's father. Jane Austen did, of course, earn some money from her writing, but her earnings were relatively small, and due to the absence of sufficient copyright protection at that time, her family received no additional money from her works after her death.

Writing novels, like teaching, was a way for women of the late eighteenth century and the early nineteenth century to earn money without losing respectability, but even novel writing was considered suspect by many. Jane Austen did not publish her novels under her own name, and few people outside the family were aware until after her death that she was a published novelist.

MRS. BENNET AND THE "BUSINESS" OF MARRIAGE

From the first line, the reader can have no doubt that marriage will be a central concern of *Pride and Prejudice*. We are told that "the business of [Mrs. Bennet's] life was to get her daughters married" (3), and we watch her throughout the novel as she schemes and plans, faces disappointments, and celebrates successes. Mrs. Bennet is foolish; she is "a woman of mean understanding, little information, and uncertain temper" (3); but she has a clear understanding of the importance of marriage for the futures of each of her five daughters. Her social ineptitude, combined with her usually inane chatter, makes her a comical character, one whose views the reader is tempted to discount altogether; but her focus on the necessity of her daughters' marrying is, in fact, reasonable, even commendable. In *Jane Austen and the State*, Mary Evans suggests that

> in view of the economic exigencies facing the unmarried daughters of the eighteenth-century gentry, Mrs. Bennet's concerns do not seem entirely ridiculous. Indeed, her obsessive concern with marriage and her ceaseless—and quite ruthless—pursuit of young men to marry her daughters are arguably instances of greater parental responsibility than the sardonic lack of interest of Mr. Bennet, to whom the activities of his wife are nothing but an irritation. (7)

Mrs. Bennet does not have the discernment to be of real help to her daughters in their search for appropriate mates, but she does understand their need to find them. The humor of Mrs. Bennet's making her daughters' marriages "the business of her life" comes from her ineptness and lack of propriety, not from her intent. At least part of the business of most women in Austen's novels is matchmaking—for themselves or for others. And that activity is only condemned within the novels when it is performed without regard for proper social decorum or despite the objections of an involved party.

Mrs. Bennet's lack of propriety is part of what concerns Mr. Darcy when he considers asking Elizabeth to marry him. Many gentlemen of the day would hesitate before acquiring a mother-in-law so little able to judge the proper behavior for specific situations and the fact that Mrs. Bennet quite obviously throws her daughters at eligible gentlemen demonstrates a gross lack of propriety. Mrs. Bennet is interested in marrying her daughters "well"—a term that in Austen's time referred almost exclusively to financial considerations. She is seen, then, as something of a fortune hunter, a quality that, unfortunately, becomes associated to some degree with even Jane and Elizabeth, the two eldest daughters—at least until the men involved become sufficiently acquainted with them to understand the differences between them and their mother.

MR. COLLINS—MARRIAGE AS A BUSINESS PROPOSITION

Like Mrs. Bennet, Mr. Collins approaches marriage as a business. It is not *the* business of his life, but it is certainly part of it. Lady Catherine de Bourgh, his benefactress, the lady of quality responsible for granting him his "living" (his position as vicar in the town of Hunsford), has "condescended to advise him to marry as soon as he could, provided he chose with discretion" (56). Since Lady Catherine believes it time for him to marry, Mr. Collins therefore determines to marry—despite the fact that there is no person within his acquaintance in whom he is interested or who appears to be interested in him. The reason for Mr. Collins's visit to his cousins at Longbourn is, in fact, to find a wife. He determines, quite reasonably if one thinks of marriage as a business enterprise, that the daughters of the man who holds the estate he will one day inherit would be eminently suitable young women from whom to choose his bride. Their social level would be acceptable; their upbringing would be likely to be in keeping with his needs as a clergyman; and they would already be familiar with and a part of the community surrounding Longbourn, which could be of value to him when he became its master.

These are not, however, the reasons Mr. Collins gives for deciding to choose one of the Bennet daughters to be his wife. Instead, he presents the goal as "his plan of amends—of atonement—for inheriting their father's estate; and he thought it an excellent one, full of eligibility and suitableness, and excessively generous and disinterested on his own part" (59). Mr. Collins thinks so highly of his plan, in fact, that he details it as part of his marriage proposal to Elizabeth:

> [B]efore I am run away with [by] my feelings on the subject, perhaps it will be advisable for me to state my reasons for marrying—and moreover for coming into Hertfordshire with the design of selecting a wife, as I certainly did. . . .
>
> My reasons for marrying are: first, that I think it a right thing for every clergyman in easy circumstances (like myself) to set the example of matrimony in his parish. Secondly, that I am convinced it will add very greatly to my happiness; and thirdly—which perhaps I ought to have mentioned earlier, that it is the particular advice and recommendation of the very noble lady whom I have the honour of calling patroness. . . . [I]t was but the very Saturday night before I left Hunsford . . . that she said, 'Mr. Collins, you must marry. A clergyman like you must marry.—chuse properly, chuse a gentlewoman for *my* sake; and for your *own*, let her be an active, useful sort of person, not brought up high, but able to make a small income go a good way. This is my advice. Find such a woman as soon as you can, bring her to Hunsford, and I will visit her.' . . . [T]he fact is, that being, as I am to inherit this estate after the death of your honoured father . . . I could not satisfy myself without resolving to chuse a wife from among his daughters, that the loss to them might be as little as possible, when the melancholy event takes place. (91)

It never occurs to Mr. Collins that Elizabeth, a young woman with a strong sense of romance and of her own worth as an individual, would not be honored by his attentions, nor that he might have better luck convincing her to marry him if he *had* allowed himself to "run away with [his] feelings on the subject." His decision to choose a wife from among his cousin's daughters might have been sound business, but sound business was not what Elizabeth wanted or expected from a marriage proposal. Mr. Collins assumes, though, that all people see (or should see) the world as he does. He cannot imagine that Elizabeth would refuse his proposal or that she would be offended by his manner of proposing. Marriage is a business to Mr. Collins just as much as it is to Mrs. Bennet. And the fact that Charlotte Lucas seeks out his proposal and accepts it with ease indicates that, even if Elizabeth (and, by inference, Austen herself) disapproves of considering marriage as business per se, such an attitude was widely accepted and openly acknowledged in Austen's time. It was acceptance of life as lived in eighteenth-century England, especially for women of the gentry and aristocracy.

CHARLOTTE LUCAS—A PRACTICAL VIEW OF MARRIAGE

Since substantial inheritances that could comfortably provide for a woman for life were rare in Austen's time, the financial future of women who never married was often bleak indeed. The prospect of spinsterhood is frightening for many of Austen's female characters. Charlotte Lucas presents perhaps the clearest picture in Austen's works of the lengths to which a woman would go to avoid the fate of spinsterhood. As the novel opens, Charlotte is twenty-seven years old, well past the age by which she had hoped to be married. She is one of several children of a former tradesman, a man who has been knighted for service to the Crown but who apparently has no significant connections or power within his community or county. Charlotte knows that her chances of marriage are constantly decreasing, and being the "sensible, intelligent young woman" (13–14) that the narrator assures us she is, she sets about creating what may well be her last opportunity to marry.

Early in the novel, even before Charlotte meets her future husband, she reveals her views about marriage to her closest friend, Elizabeth:

> Happiness in marriage is entirely a matter of chance. If the dispositions of the parties are ever so well known to each other, or ever so similar before-hand, it does not advance their felicity in the least. They always contrive to grow sufficiently unlike afterwards to have their share of vexation; and it is better to know as little as possible of the defects of the person with whom you are to pass your life. (18)

The younger and less jaded Elizabeth claims that Charlotte herself " 'would never act in this way' " (18). But Elizabeth is wrong. Charlotte adheres to her own words, and both her indirect wooing of Elizabeth's rejected suitor and her acceptance of his marriage proposal demonstrate just how threatened Miss Lucas feels by the spectre of spinsterhood. She is willing to make herself attractive to an obsequious, pompous, wife-seeking man merely because he is able to provide a home and security for her. She does not care that the marriage will not be based on love and personal devotion. Financial security, a home of her own, and a respectable position in the community are sufficient to draw her into marriage. She chooses to become a good wife to Mr. Collins, one who brings favor to him in his community and manages his home willingly and competently. She never, however, finds him as companionable as one might wish to find a husband, as becomes clear from her choice of a sitting room. Elizabeth notes that Charlotte has chosen a back room of the parsonage for personal entertainment. When visiting the Collinses, Elizabeth at first

> rather wondered that Charlotte should not prefer the dining parlour for common use; it was a better sized room, and had a pleasanter aspect; but she soon saw that her friend had an excellent reason for what she did, for Mr. Collins would undoubtedly have been much less in his own apartment, had they sat in one equally lively; and she gave Charlotte credit for the arrangement. (144)

This perspective is Elizabeth's, not Charlotte's, but it is certainly a reasonable one, and supports Elizabeth's assumption that Charlotte does not enjoy the constant company of her husband. That Charlotte never directly reveals her feelings about her husband demonstrates how clearly she understands what propriety requires of her. As Mr. Collins's wife, Charlotte never says a word that could be taken negatively about him. She does not complain about her situation or question aloud her decision to marry him. She never feigns passionate affection, but she never indicates dissatisfaction either. She is a proper, prudent, and respectable vicar's wife whose inner life the reader is never allowed to see.

Charlotte's age at the time of her marriage, twenty-seven, is an important one for women in Austen's fiction. It is the age at which *Sense and Sensibility*'s Marianne Dashwood (who is, at the time, considerably younger) supposes that if a woman's " 'home be un-comfortable, or her fortune small . . . she might bring herself to submit to the offices of a nurse [for an aging husband], for the sake of the provision and security of a wife' " (32). In other words, it is the age at which Marianne assumes that a woman might give up on love and sell herself into a marriage of convenience. It is also the age at which *Persuasion*'s Anne Elliot, who a "few years before" had been "a very pretty girl," has lost her "bloom" and, presumably, her chances of being advantageously married (12). And it is the age at which the author herself precipitately accepted a proposal of marriage from a man whose sisters she was visiting— an acceptance that she was to take back less than twenty-four hours later. The age of twenty-seven then, for Austen, appears to have been a line of demarcation between the periods of likely marriage-ability and likely spinsterhood in a woman's life. Upon reaching this age, whatever dreams Charlotte Lucas might have had about finding a husband with whom she could share a romantic life had ended, and she was determinedly practical, making it the business of her own life to marry prudently and create a secure home and future for herself through marriage.

MR. BENNET

Whereas Mrs. Bennet is incapable of acting effectively on behalf of her daughters, Mr. Bennet has the capacity, but not the will, to provide for their future intelligently and effectively. He behaves irresponsibly toward both his estate and his dependents. He does not lack intelligence or an understanding of human nature, but he does not have a strong belief in the need to act according to prin-ciple and moral obligation. Instead, he operates as an observer, watching what happens around him and returning to his study whenever life gets too uncomfortable for him. Without a diligent regard for principled action, Mr. Bennet, for all his intelligence and his insight into the natures of those around him, cannot and does not act ethically and effectively as the head of his family. He po-sitions himself as a somewhat unattached observer of his family's foibles rather than as the example of ethical propriety and action to his family that his position demands of him.

The Bennets, as "the principal inhabitants" of the neighborhood of Longbourn, are, though only middle-level gentry in income and power, the dominant family permanently in residence. Others, like the Lucases, may have titles, but the family at Longbourn is longer established and, as a result of their longer tenure, has greater social currency. As the head of such a family, Mr. Bennet would generally be expected to set an example for his neighborhood: possibly to act as a magistrate and certainly to recognize the importance of holding positions of authority within both home and neighborhood. In fact, however, he rarely concerns himself with issues of authority in the community or the home, retreating instead to the privacy and personal safety of his library at the very moments in which effective, intelligent authority is most needed by his family.

Mr. Bennet's impotence when Lydia elopes with Wickham is a direct result of his irresponsible behavior as the head of his family, both in his failure to provide his daughters with an example of propriety and responsible behavior within the family unit and in living to the extent of his income. Because he has not set aside money for his daughters' futures, he must rely on others to salvage Lydia's reputation and provide for all of his daughters' futures.

The narrator is quite explicit about Mr. Bennet's failure to be an example of propriety in the home. We are assured that

> [h]ad Elizabeth's opinion been all drawn from her own family, she could not have formed a very pleasing picture of conjugal felicity or domestic comfort. Her father, captivated by youth and beauty, and that appearance of good humour, which youth and beauty generally give, had married a woman whose weak understanding and illiberal mind, had very early in their marriage put an end to all real affection for her. Respect, esteem, and confidence, had vanished for ever; and all his views of domestic happiness were overthrown. . . . To his wife he was very little otherwise indebted, than as her ignorance and folly had contributed to his amusement. (202)

To choose a wife merely on the basis of youth and beauty without paying attention to the weakness of her understanding or the illiberality of her mind is an error made by characters in several of Austen's novels. Such a choice displays the poor judgment of the man in his youth. But the condemnation of Mr. Bennet goes beyond his making a poor choice in his youth. Instead of making the best of the situation, perhaps by attempting to educate his wife and creating an environment of respect between them, he entertains himself with her "ignorance and folly." Such is not the action of an ethical and compassionate husband, nor is it behavior fitting for a proper head of the family in Austen's fiction.

Mr. Bennet's disrespectful actions toward his wife affect his daughters as well:

> Elizabeth . . . had never been blind to the impropriety of her father's
> behaviour as a husband. She had always seen it with pain; but re-
> specting his abilities, and grateful for his affectionate treatment of
> herself, she endeavoured to forget what she could not overlook,
> and to banish from her thoughts that continual breach of conjugal
> obligation and decorum which, in exposing his wife to the contempt
> of her own children, was so highly reprehensible. (203)

Elizabeth recognizes that her father's behavior offends propriety.
She, with her superior understanding, sees her father's errors. His
bad example does not, therefore, negatively affect her own behavior. But her sister Lydia, a young girl fascinated by the uniforms of
the militia regiment and flattered by the attention and attractiveness of Wickham, is easy prey for the disreputable young soldier.
Just as Mr. Bennet was "captivated by youth and beauty" in his
own choice of a mate, so is Lydia captivated by Wickham. The fact
that Wickham has no intention of marrying Lydia makes her choice
potentially much more disastrous than her father's, but the choices
themselves have much in common.

Mr. Bennet could have prevented his daughter's disgrace if he
had been more active in directing his household's activities. When
Lydia is invited to go to Brighton with the regiment, Elizabeth asks
her father to forbid it, reminding him of Lydia's susceptibility. To
forbid her going, however, would put him at odds with both his
wife and Lydia, and he chooses not to trouble himself by taking
such action. In Brighton Lydia is free from even the minor restraints that are placed upon her actions at home and can behave
as impetuously and improperly as she chooses.

That Austen sets Lydia's ruin in Brighton with the militia comments very particularly on a specific social situation of her time.
Brighton was one of the favorite playgrounds of the Prince Regent,
whose lack of propriety, decorum, and moral behavior was leg-
endary. Many of the militia were stationed at or near Brighton, in
fact, because of the frequent presence of the Prince Regent and
Mrs. Fitzherbert, his wife/mistress, at their lodgings in Brighton.
(Mrs. Fitzherbert and the Prince went through a secret marriage
ceremony, but the marriage was invalid, as the Prince Regent knew
at the time. He eventually disregarded the invalid marriage to Mrs.
Fitzherbert and married someone acceptable to the government.)
Austen, like many of her contemporaries, highly disapproved of

the Prince Regent's public and private behavior. Her letters indicate her displeasure not only at his behavior itself but at the example it set. Thus, the fact that Wickham elopes with Lydia from Brighton, intending to enjoy her favors without the benefit of marriage (though she seems to expect to be married—as did the Prince Regent's mistress), would inevitably remind Austen's initial readers of what many perceived to be the accelerated moral decline of the leaders of Great Britain, as well as convey Mr. Bennet's ineffectiveness as a father. If Elizabeth can perceive the danger that Brighton poses to Lydia, her father should be able to perceive it as well. But he chooses instead to retreat to his library and allow Lydia and her mother to have their way.

Once Lydia has eloped with Wickham, the only possibility of salvaging her reputation is through persuading him to marry her. The primary responsibility for the search for the lovers and the negotiations with the young man would, by rights, fall to the head of the young woman's family. But again, Mr. Bennet cannot act effectively. Initially he goes in search of the pair, but he is unable to find them, or even to put together a reasonable plan for doing so. Mr. Gardiner, his brother-in-law, quickly takes control of both the search and the negotiations once the pair are discovered. Mr. Bennet retires to the peaceful refuge of his library to await the outcome. He does not, however, excuse himself entirely. He recognizes that his impotence in the situation is the direct result of his financial and ethical irresponsibility as a father and head of the family estate:

> Had he done his duty . . . Lydia need not have been indebted to her uncle, for whatever of honour or credit could now be purchased for her. The satisfaction of prevailing on one of the most worthless young men in Great Britain to be her husband, might then have rested on its proper place. (263)

The "proper place" for such negotiations is in the hands of the young woman's father. Therefore, Lydia's debt to her uncle, who intercedes on her behalf, is indeed great. He has convinced Wickham to marry her by offering money and the purchase of a commission in the army, thus buying "whatever of honour or credit" was possible for her after the elopement. For an uncle to negotiate in such a way for a fatherless girl (or even for the daughter of a man who is subordinate within the family hierarchy) would be in accordance with propriety, but that the uncle finds it necessary to do so when the father is both alive and the presiding head of the family demonstrates Mr. Bennet's inadequacy to act on his family's behalf.

Mr. Bennet deeply regrets his need to rely on his brother-in-law to resolve the Lydia/Wickham affair, but at least, he believes, the problem has remained within the family, and therefore some degree of propriety has been maintained. In fact, his assumptions are false. Mr. Darcy, a man with no familial attachment to the Bennets (despite his once having proposed to Elizabeth, a fact unknown to the family), has provided Mr. Gardiner with the money necessary to buy Wickham off. Darcy's reasons are logical and, when they are revealed, make sense to the reader as well as to Elizabeth and her family, but that fact does not obscure Mr. Bennet's inability to handle the affairs of his own household. His neglect of his responsibilities as the head of the family has injured his daughters, and it is mere chance that they have friends willing and able to help them out of their difficulties and to marry them despite their family's shortcomings. Elizabeth is correct in her evaluation of her father's behavior. There are indeed considerable "disadvantages which must attend the children of so unsuitable a marriage" and real "evils arising from so ill-judged a direction of [her father's] talents; talents which rightly used, might at least have preserved the respectability of his daughters" (203). That the eldest two Bennet girls grow into such reasonable, attractive, and morally upright women is more a matter of inherent goodness or luck than of upbringing. Neither parent has provided them with an example of propriety and responsible behavior meriting emulation.

MR. DARCY

When the reader first meets Fitzwilliam Darcy, he is twenty-eight years old and far from home, where he offends all but his closest friends with what his new acquaintances consider to be excessive pride. The narrator informs us: "Darcy was clever. He was at the same time haughty, reserved, and fastidious, and his manners, though well bred, were not inviting" (12). By setting Darcy in this context, Austen accomplishes two objectives. First, she provides circumstances that will more easily present his flaws than his virtues at the outset of the story; second, she prevents the reader (and the other characters in the novel who are meeting him for the first time) from judging him on the basis of anything but his own superficial behavior. The initial conclusions about Darcy reached by Elizabeth and the others in the neighborhood of Netherfield are, as a result, based only on superficial facts and behavior, not on a firm understanding of the man. The outer pridefulness perceived in Darcy by the neighborhood of Netherfield causes him to be judged unfairly. The people of the neighborhood, due to their lack of knowledge about his upbringing, his family situation, and his past behavior, are biased against him from the outset. Instead of judging him fairly, they prejudge, preferring attractive, good-humored, well-spoken young men like Mr. Bingley and Mr. Wickham over a man of substance like Mr. Darcy who is not so easygoing and who does not see fit to court their favor.

The fact that Mr. Darcy is basically a good, solid man of substance, ethically as well as financially, does not, however, excuse his behavior in all circumstances. Even he admits that his demeanor is often prideful and his behavior selfish. Near the end of the novel, he tries to explain to Elizabeth the reasons for his prideful behavior:

> I have been a selfish being all my life, in practice, though not in principle. As a child I was taught what was *right*, but I was not taught to correct my temper. I was given good principles, but left to follow them in pride and conceit. Unfortunately an only son, (for many years an only *child*) I was spoilt by my parents, who though good themselves, (my father particularly, all that was benevolent and amiable,) allowed, encouraged, almost taught me to be selfish and overbearing, to care for none beyond my own family circle, to think meanly of all the rest of the world, to *wish* at least to think meanly of their sense and worth compared with my own. Such I was, from eight to eight and twenty. (319)

His father's indulgence of Darcy's selfishness and conceit has allowed the latter to grow into the proud young man we meet at Netherfield. But Darcy's father was also a good role model for his son, being " 'all that was benevolent and amiable.' " When Darcy is on his home territory, he takes on his father's qualities of benevolence and amiability, overcomes the excesses of pride he displays in other surroundings, and behaves as a good master and landlord to the people he is responsible for as the owner of Pemberley.

Mrs. Reynolds, the housekeeper at Pemberley, speaks glowingly of her young master: " 'I have never had a cross word from him in my life, and I have known him ever since he was four years old' " (210). To Mr. Gardiner's remark that she is " 'lucky in having such a master,' " Mrs. Reynolds replies: " 'Yes, Sir, I know I am. If I was to go through the world, I could not meet with a better. But I have always observed, that they who are good-natured when children, are good-natured when they grow up; and he was always the sweetest-tempered, most generous-hearted, boy in the world' " (211).

In light of Darcy's later evaluation of his selfishness from the age of eight to twenty-eight, we might be inclined (with Elizabeth and the Gardiners) to doubt the veracity of the housekeeper's judgment. But Mrs. Reynolds has known Darcy since he was a boy, has an understanding of his history, and has judged him based on lengthy observation and considerable evidence. She admits that " '[s]ome people call him proud,' " but she claims never to have seen " 'any thing of it' " (211). Instead, she claims that " '[h]e is the best landlord, and the best master . . . that ever lived. Not like the wild young men now-a-days, who think of nothing but themselves. There is not one of his tenants or servants but what will give him a good name' " (211).

Darcy is considered proud by those, including Elizabeth, who are prejudiced against him. Samuel Johnson, in his 1755 *Dictionary of the English Language,* defines "prejudice" as a "prepossession; a judgement formed beforehand without examination." It is only people who make conclusions based on superficial facts (most of those in the neighborhood of Longbourn) and those who intentionally skew the facts to suit their own ends (Mr. Wickham, for example) who consider Mr. Darcy to be too proud; those who know him best know better.

If, however, Darcy's pride is a matter of perspective, what about his prejudice? Certainly he is prejudged by those in the neighborhood of Longbourn, but is he free from prejudice himself? Darcy's prejudice is actually more of a failing than his pride. Like Elizabeth, he forms his judgments "beforehand without examination." The fact that some of Darcy's prejudices (such as those against Mr. and

Mrs. Bennet), when examined, are retained as reasoned judgments should not blind us to the fact that they begin as unfounded, unexamined assumptions about people based on their social position, the restrictions of geography, and their financial circumstances.

Darcy's automatic response to finding out that Jane and Elizabeth's uncles are a Meryton attorney and a Cheapside tradesman is that it " 'must very materially lessen their chance of marrying men of any consideration in the world' " (30). This statement indicates his prejudice against the nonlanded classes of society, not merely because he makes it (it is, in fact, a true statement in a stratified society deeply concerned with property), but because of the context in which he makes it. Mr. Bingley is obviously falling in love with Jane Bennet at this point in the novel, and Darcy, along with Bingley's sisters, determines to prevent him from marrying a woman with connections so much lower socially than his own. In reality, however, the connections that Darcy uses as examples of the Bennets' social inferiority here are not inferior to Bingley's own. Bingley's fortune has come from trade, and he is, in fact, the first generation of his family to be able to lead the life of a leisured gentleman. Bingley is not old family or old money. He does not even have a family seat (unlike the Bennets, whose family seat, Longbourn, may be modest but has existed for generations). Bingley's predecessors have made a larger fortune than the Bennets', but they belonged to a lower social level. Darcy's comment on the Bennets' disadvantageous connections indicates a lack of examined judgment. He reacts automatically to the situation, judging human beings on their immediate relative social and financial position rather than looking at the moral worth of the specific individuals involved.

Later in the novel, when he feels the need to explain to Elizabeth his objections to the inferiority of her connections, his reasoning changes significantly. By this point, having fallen in love with Elizabeth and as a result having a vested interest in her situation, he has revised his opinion based on his expanded view of her connections. No longer is the fact of her uncles' less-than-genteel sources of income the main issue; now the issue is her immediate family's lack of propriety: " 'The situation of your mother's family, though objectionable, was nothing in comparison of that total want of propriety so frequently, so almost uniformly betrayed by herself, by your three younger sisters, and occasionally even by your father' " (169–70). Darcy's judgment here is much more considered and reasonable than the prejudice he displayed earlier to make the same point about the inferiority of the Bennet girls' connections. The "objectionable" nature of Elizabeth's connections is no longer based exclusively on social and business considerations; rather it is now based on the respectability (or lack thereof) of the behavior of those of her connections he has observed at close range. This judgment is fair and accurate, and Elizabeth understands his initial reaction to her family when he explains it this way.

Yet we must remember that Darcy's objection was not always a matter of reasoned judgment. Only in the course of the novel does he learn to judge Elizabeth's family accurately rather than to indulge in unexamined prejudices about them. Probably the biggest surprise of his marriage to Elizabeth is the relationship he develops with her aunt and uncle Gardiner, the tradesman from Cheapside. These connections, whom Darcy once thought likely to prevent the Bennet girls from marrying well because of their inferior social status, actually become Darcy's close friends.

Such a change in Darcy's attitude toward the Gardiners seems to indicate a growth of understanding within him of the nature of prejudice, but Austen doesn't actually provide us with that reassurance. Darcy has always been capable of judging the individual case when it is within the realm of his personal interest and influence. He recognizes Bingley's innate goodness and is attracted to it despite the fact that Bingley's social position is substantially lower than his own; he recognizes Lady Catherine's excessive pride and inordinate prejudice despite the ties of blood; he recognizes Wickham's lack of integrity despite the obligations of his family toward Wickham's father. In order to be convinced that Darcy has learned to distrust prejudice in general, the reader would need to see his actions in situations in which his personal and family interests are not involved. Austen does not present us with such a situation near the end of the novel. Thus, we cannot be certain that Darcy has freed himself from prejudice in his interactions with society at large. He does, however, seem to become more able to step back and examine his assumptions in the face of fact, and not to act automatically upon his initial impressions.

ELIZABETH BENNET

Although Mr. Darcy is guilty of prejudice in some of his judgments, the major character most susceptible to prejudice in the novel is Elizabeth. If the primary eighteenth-century definition of prejudice is a "prepossession; a judgement formed beforehand without examination," then prejudice is Elizabeth's greatest failing.

At the beginning of the novel, Elizabeth shares the judgment of Darcy formed by the rest of the neighborhood people when he refuses to dance with or even to be introduced to any woman he does not already know. The narrator informs us that "he was discovered to be proud, to be above his company, and above being pleased" (7). Before the evening was over, "[h]is character was decided. He was the proudest, most disagreeable man in the world, and every body hoped that he would never come there again" (7–8). Elizabeth, having been slighted by Darcy's not asking her to dance and having been influenced by the general attitude toward Darcy, assumes that he is indeed proud beyond seemliness and that he is not worthy of her attention. Thus, when she later notices that his eyes are frequently "fixed on her," she is confused about what to make of it:

> She hardly knew how to suppose that she could be an object of admiration to so great a man; and yet that he should look at her because he disliked her, was still more strange. She could only imagine however at last, that she drew his notice because there was a something about her more wrong and reprehensible, according to his ideas of right, than in any other person present. This supposition did not pain her. She liked him too little to care for his approbation. (42)

The perceptive reader understands that, in fact, Elizabeth *does* "care for his approbation," even if she is unwilling to admit it, even to herself, at this point in the story. If she did not care, she wouldn't even notice the attention he paid her.

Later, upon hearing Wickham's version of the story of his mistreatment by Darcy, Elizabeth accepts it, based solely on the fact that Wickham is more sociable and more enjoyable company than Darcy has been. Wickham tells his story convincingly, but there is no evidence beyond Wickham's word to indicate Darcy's culpability. Elizabeth, however, does not examine the facts; she does not consider that her acquaintance with Wickham is of even shorter duration than her acquaintance with Darcy, nor the fact that Wickham has no friends of long acquaintance nearby to vouch for his character, whereas Darcy travels in the company of Bingley and his family, who have known and admired him for many years. Elizabeth believes Wickham's story of Darcy's infamy, based solely on Wickham's outer appearance of goodness and Darcy's appearing proud.

Only after Elizabeth has read Darcy's letter detailing Wickham's most wicked improprieties does she begin to question her earlier judgment, but the questioning does not come easily even then. She first read Darcy's letter with "a strong prejudice against every thing he might say" (175). And that prejudice was difficult for her to overcome.

> [W]hen she read . . . a relation of events, which, if true, must overthrow every cherished opinion of [Wickham's] worth, and which bore so alarming an affinity to his own history of himself, her apprehension, and even horror, oppressed her. She wished to discredit it entirely, repeatedly exclaiming, "This must be false! This cannot be! This must be the grossest falsehood!"—and when she had gone through the whole letter, though scarcely knowing any thing of the last page or two, put it hastily away, protesting that she would not regard it, that she would never look in it again. (175)

Elizabeth does look at the letter again, and she begins to reconstruct Wickham's words and behavior, examining aspects of them in ways that make her doubt her own judgment more fully than ever:

> She perfectly remembered every thing that had passed in conversation between Wickham and herself, in their first evening at Mr. Philips's. Many of his expressions were still fresh in her memory. She was *now* struck with the impropriety of such communications to a stranger, and wondered it had escaped her before. She saw the indelicacy of putting himself forward as he had done, and the inconsistency of his professions with his conduct. She remembered that he had boasted of having no fear of seeing Mr. Darcy—that Mr. Darcy might leave the country, but that *he* should stand his ground; yet he had avoided the Netherfield ball the very next week. She

remembered also, that till the Netherfield family had quitted the country, he had told his story to no one but herself; but that after their removal, it had been every where discussed; that he had then no reserves, no scruples in sinking Mr. Darcy's character, though he had assured her that respect for the father, would always prevent his exposing the son.

How differently did every thing now appear in which he was concerned. (177)

Elizabeth wants to cling to her initial judgments, but she is forced, through examining the facts of the matter, to recognize her own shortcomings.

She grew absolutely ashamed of herself.—Of neither Darcy nor Wickham could she think without feeling that she had been blind, partial, prejudiced, absurd.

"How despicably have I acted!" she cried.—"I, who have prided myself on my discernment!—I, who have valued myself on my abilities! . . . Pleased with the preference of one, and offended by the neglect of the other, on the very beginning of our acquaintance, I have courted prepossession and ignorance, and driven reason away, where either were concerned. Till this moment, I never knew myself." (178)

Elizabeth recognizes her "prepossession," her tendency to rush to judgment without a fair and close examination of the available evidence. She acknowledges her tendency toward prejudice, of choosing to believe what flatters her and to resist what she finds offensive, even when it is true. Elizabeth's pride in her discernment has, in fact, been prideful and vain prejudice. It is only when she comes to recognize this quality in herself and begins to take steps to eradicate it that she is able to mature into the strong young woman we see at the end of the novel.

Elizabeth grows, in the course of the novel, from a young woman who prejudges most people and behaviors based on their most obvious outward appearances to a young wife who thinks before she speaks, who checks herself when tempted to laugh at a husband who "had yet to learn to be laught at" (321), who recognizes both the virtues and the flaws of the people around her, and who loves the people she loves for their innermost selves. She grows from a girl who is determinedly proud of the discernment she mistakenly believes she possesses (a discernment based on prejudice) into a thoughtful, caring woman of true discernment.

CONCLUSION

Pride and Prejudice is a love story, but it is much more. It is a story about personal responsibility and moral obligation in a world that, like our own, seems to many to be disintegrating ethically. Darcy and Elizabeth learn, in the course of the novel, how to make decisions based on clear and fair judgments of evidence, combined with a sense of responsible and ethical behavior toward family and friends. They do not choose to satisfy their own desires at the expense of others, but work to make right what is wrong in the lives of those they love, even at personal cost. Finally, seemingly as a reward for their behaving in accordance with both an internal sense of ethics and an external world of proprieties, they are able to marry and to continue to grow happily together as man and wife.

Punishment and reward are not necessarily meted out equally, though. Lydia gets her husband, and Mrs. Bennet seems as pleased to have Wickham for a son-in-law as she is to have Bingley and Darcy. The reader is told that Lydia and Wickham will always tend to be in debt and that their passion will cool, but there is no indication that their marriage will be less happy than most marriages of the period. Thus Lydia and Wickham are not treated by the novel as the traditional fallen woman/rogue combination. Instead, they are treated as two people, raised in families where parenting is ineffective and moral examples are not the strongest, who lose their way in a world that sometimes seems to reward immorality, even among those who hold the highest positions in the land.

Austen does not present simple solutions to what are, in fact, complex problems. Marriage for the sake of money is disapproved of; yet Charlotte Lucas and Mr. Collins marry for security and convenience, and both seem to be content with their choice. Chastity is considered essential to respectability; yet Lydia seems to recover her respectability; even though everyone knows that she lived with Wickham before her marriage. Mr. Bennet's failings as a father could cause his daughters to be left in penury and in disrepute, but by the end of the novel three of them are married, two very successfully in both financial and moral terms, and the third has recovered from potential moral and physical ruin. Dealing with issues of love, money, and proper behavior in the real world is complicated today, as it was two centuries ago. In *Pride and Prejudice*, Austen presents the issues in all their complexity and, in the characters of Elizabeth and Darcy, Jane and Bingley, demonstrates that, despite the complications and temptations of the world, ethically responsible behavior serves everyone, even those who seem at times to be giving up their own desires in order to adhere to it. Those who do not follow propriety and personal responsibility may not always be punished, but those who do are compensated by more than material rewards.

TOPICS FOR WRITTEN OR ORAL EXPLORATION

1. Choose one of the minor characters in *Pride and Prejudice* (one for whom the novel does not provide extensive details about upbringing, etc.). Write a character study in which you analyze his or her character as it is presented in the novel and then invent a history that would account for the way he or she behaves. Be able to defend the history that you create. Possible subjects for the analysis include Mr. Collins, Lady Catherine de Bourgh, Anne de Bourgh, Mr. Bingley, Miss Bingley, Mr. or Mrs. Hurst, Colonel Fitzwilliam, and Charlotte Lucas.

2. Write an essay on the importance of propriety in *Pride and Prejudice*.

3. Write an essay on the importance of property in *Pride and Prejudice*.

4. Choose one of the letters in the novel and analyze it to demonstrate how the language as well as the content indicates the character's state of mind at the time it was written.

5. Imagine life for the characters five years after the close of the novel. Write a description of the lives of each of the following families five years later:

The Darcys	The Bingleys
The Wickhams	The Bennets
The Collinses	The de Bourghs

6. Write an essay explaining why, how, and when Elizabeth fell in love with Darcy. Be sure to use details from the novel to support your point of view.

7. Write an essay explaining why, how, and when Darcy fell in love with Elizabeth. Be sure to use details from the novel to support your point of view.

8. Divide the class into two groups, one to argue for practical marriage (à la Charlotte Lucas) and the other to argue for romantic marriage (à la Elizabeth Bennet). Initiate a debate in which you examine the pros and cons of both positions.

9. Choose passages from three different places in the novel that display the irony of the narrator. Discuss what about the language used indicates the irony and how that irony contributes to your interpretation of the novel.

10. Why did Elizabeth not tell her family about Wickham's behavior with Darcy's sister? Do you think she was right at the time not to tell them? Consider the ethics of the situation from all angles in an essay.

11. Discuss the following: To what extent are the faults of the Bennet daughters the result of their parents' failures as parents? To what extent are the virtues of the Bennet daughters the result of their parents' successful parenting? To what extent does each Bennet daughter have to take responsibility for her own positive or negative behavior?

12. Write an essay on the theme of personal responsibility in the novel.

13. Write an essay on the theme of familial obligation in the novel.

14. Write an essay explaining why the values that *Pride and Prejudice* supports would or would not be appropriate values for people to hold as we enter the twenty-first century.

15. View one or more film versions of *Pride and Prejudice*. Discuss the choices the director made in creating the film. Write an essay in which you analyze the relative success or failure of the film version(s) you watched in terms of faithfulness to the novel.

SUGGESTED READINGS

Armstrong, Nancy. *Desire and Domestic Fiction: A Political History of the Novel*. New York: Oxford University Press, 1987.

Austen, Jane. *Persuasion*. Oxford: Oxford University Press, 1971.

———. *Pride and Prejudice*. London: J. M. Dent and Sons, 1906.

———. *Sense and Sensibility*. Oxford: Oxford University Press, 1990.

Brophy, Elizabeth Bergen. *Women's Lives and the Eighteenth-Century English Novel*. Tampa: University of South Florida Press, 1991.

Brown, Julia Prewitt. *Jane Austen's Novels: Social Change and Literary Form*. Cambridge, MA: Harvard University Press, 1979.

Brown, Lloyd W. "The Business of Marrying and Mothering." In *Jane Austen's Achievement*. Edited by Juliet McMaster. London: Macmillan, 1976. 27–43.

Butler, Marilyn. *Jane Austen and the War of Ideas*. Oxford: Clarendon Press, 1975.

———. *Romantics, Rebels and Reactionaries: English Literature and Its Background 1760–1830*. Oxford: Oxford University Press, 1981.

Evans, Mary. *Jane Austen and the State*. London: Tavistock Press, 1987.

Fergus, Jan S. *Jane Austen and the Didactic Novel*. London: Macmillan, 1983.

Grey, J. David, ed. *The Jane Austen Companion*. New York: Macmillan, 1986.

Hardy, Barbara. "Property and Possessions in Jane Austen's Novels." In *Jane Austen's Achievement*. Edited by Juliet McMaster. London: Macmillan, 1976. 79–105.

Hunter, J. Paul. *Before Novels: The Cultural Contexts of Eighteenth-Century English Fiction*. New York: W. W. Norton, 1990.

Johnson, Claudia L. *Jane Austen: Women, Politics, and the Novel*. Chicago: University of Chicago Press, 1988.

Mews, Hazel. *Frail Vessels: Woman's Role in Women's Novels from Fanny Burney to George Eliot*. London: Athlone, 1969.

Miles, Rosalind. *The Female Form: Women Writers and the Conquest of the Novel*. London: Routledge and Kegan Paul, 1987.

Monaghan, David, ed. *Jane Austen in a Social Context*. Totowa, NJ: Barnes and Noble, 1981.

Mudrick, Marvin. *Jane Austen: Irony as Defense and Discovery*. Princeton, NJ: Princeton University Press, 1952.

Nardin, Jane. *Those Elegant Decorums: The Concept of Propriety in Jane Austen's Novels*. Albany: SUNY Press, 1973.

Nussbaum, Felicity, and Laura Brown, eds. *The New Eighteenth Century: Theory, Poetics, English Literature*. New York: Methuen, 1987.

Perry, Ruth. *Women, Letters and the Novel*. New York: AMS Press, 1980.

Poovey, Mary. *The Proper Lady and the Woman Writer: Ideology as Style in the Works of Mary Wollstonecraft, Mary Shelley, and Jane Austen*. Chicago: University of Chicago Press, 1984.

Rogers, Pat, ed. *The Eighteenth Century*. London: Methuen, 1978.

————. *Literature and Popular Culture in Eighteenth Century England*. Totowa, NJ: Barnes and Noble, 1985.

Ruderman, Anne Crippen. *The Pleasures of Virtue: Political Thought in the Novels of Jane Austen*. Lanham, MD: Rowman and Littlefield, 1995.

Scholfield, Mary Anne, and Cecilia Macheski, eds. *Fettr'd or Free? British Women Novelists, 1670–1815*. Athens: Ohio University Press, 1986.

Spencer, Jane. *The Rise of the Woman Novelist*. Oxford: Basil Blackwell, 1986.

Stewart, Maaja A. *Domestic Realities and Imperial Fictions: Jane Austen's Novels in Eighteenth-Century Contexts*. Athens: University of Georgia Press, 1993.

Sulloway, Alison G. *Jane Austen and the Province of Womanhood*. Philadelphia: University of Pennsylvania Press, 1988.

Tanner, Tony. *Jane Austen*. Cambridge, MA: Harvard University Press, 1986.

Todd, Janet M. *Women's Friendship in Literature: The Eighteenth-Century Novel in England and France*. New York: Columbia University Press, 1980.

Watt, Ian, ed. *Jane Austen: A Collection of Critical Essays*. Englewood Cliffs, NJ: Prentice-Hall, 1963.

2

Law and Custom:
Inheritance and Marriage

PROPERTY LAW AND INHERITANCE

The world of *Pride and Prejudice*, as in all of Jane Austen's novels, is founded on the principle of property that determined much of the social and economic activity of late eighteenth- and early nineteenth-century England. In this society one's possessions (particularly real estate) and one's personal and family connections were intricately interconnected. One's house was not merely the building in which one lived or even a collection of buildings one owned; instead, one's house included lineage (ancestry and descent) and collateral relations (cousins, nephews, etc.) as well as the estate or estates belonging to that lineage. In fact, one of the definitions of the word "house" in Samuel Johnson's 1755 *Dictionary of the English Language* is "family of ancestors, descendants, and kindred; race."

The "house" of a British aristocratic or gentry family generally had only one primary leader at a given time. Because of general adherence to the practice of primogeniture within British society, the head of house role within the family was usually filled by the eldest living male in the main line of descent. Thus, Darcy, filling that position in his family, is the head of his house; Colonel Fitzwilliam, not in the direct line of descent, is considered subordinate to Darcy in family matters. This subordination does not mean that Darcy does not ask advice and assistance from his cousin; however, Darcy's decisions regarding family properties and behavior carry considerably more weight than those of his cousin.

Primogeniture, basically the inheritance of a father's estate by the eldest son of a family, was both law and custom in eighteenth- and nineteenth-century England. Under common law (the foundation of most law in both England and the United States), if a man died intestate (without a will), his property passed to his eldest son. If he had no son, the property was left to his daughters in equal portions. If his wife was still alive, under the law she received a portion (generally one-third of the estate) which she could use to support herself for the rest of her life; upon her death, that portion of the estate would revert to his heir or heirs (his eldest son or his daughters).

In fact, however, few families with substantial landed property (real estate as opposed to personal estate) let its distribution be determined by common law. Few men of property died intestate; instead, many made wills that determined the distribution of all that they owned outright after death; and an even larger number had to adhere to contracts known as "strict settlements" or "entails," which gave them no say in how the family estate would be distributed after their death. The strict settlement, or entail, is the legal device that places the Bennet daughters in such precarious financial circumstances; under its terms, Mr. Bennet's estate will be inherited not by his daughters (as it would under the common law application of primogeniture) but by a distant male cousin, Mr. Collins.

Under strict settlement, the head of the family lived on the property, collected income from it and the other family investments, and was responsible for the maintenance and care of the physical estate and most, if not all, other sources of family income. He was not, however, the true *owner* of the estate. Instead, he held the position of life tenant, holding the estate in trust for the next generation. As A.W.B. Simpson points out in his 1986 *History of the Land Law*,

the whole history of [strict] settlements can only be made intelligible if we remember that although the family as such was not treated as a legal entity by the common law, which dealt only in individual property rights, landed society did nevertheless view property as ultimately belonging to the family in some moral sense, and the legal system reflected this. (209)

Thus, the strict settlement was set up as a way to preserve the estate for the benefit of the family at large, to protect it against the desires of a single owner who might use it to his advantage but to the detriment of the family as a whole.

The principle of primogeniture, the concentrating of inheritance in the male line of descent, is customarily taken to even stronger extremes in strict settlement than it is under common law. Whereas under common law a man's estate was inherited either by his eldest son or by his daughters as equal partners, under strict settlement estates were often left to men in more distant branches of the family rather than to the daughters of the life tenant. Such is the case with the Bennet estate. The strict settlement made upon Longbourn means that, since Mr. Bennet has no son, it will pass to the nearest male relative in another branch of the family (a collateral male). Thus, strict settlement, while created in part to limit the detrimental effects of primogeniture on the family at large, encourages male inheritance of estates even more fully than primogeniture under the common law does.

The primary purpose of the strict settlement was to protect the estate throughout time. The strict settlement was usually set up in such a way as to encourage the heir (the second generation), in whose trust the life tenant held the estate, to settle the estate on *his* future heir (the third generation) before being able to take possession of the property, making the heir (the second generation) the next life tenant rather than ever allowing him to come into full ownership of the property. Thus, the family's interest remained protected through multiple generations by keeping physical possession of the estate and actual ownership of it in separate hands, thereby restricting the uses to which the estate and the estate moneys could be put by any single person.

For example, a person who owned an estate free and clear would have the right to use any and all portions of it in whatever ways he chose: he could cut down woods and sell the timber; he could sell portions of the land itself to people looking for small plots in the country; he could tear down buildings at will or put up inferior new buildings that might decrease the value of the estate as a whole. As a life tenant, however, his powers were limited. Because he held the estate in trust for a future generation, he was legally responsible for maintaining it intact for that future generation. Thus, while he might be allowed to cut and sell a small amount of timber on the estate to meet expenses, he would not be allowed to denude the estate of trees for personal profit. While he might be allowed to build new buildings or to tear down old ones, he would have to be able to provide reasonable proof that his actions improved the estate, raising its value for the next generation. Otherwise, he could be held responsible for the difference in value between the estate as it would have been before his changes to it and its value after.

Strict settlements often included provisions for the financial care of widows of deceased heads of houses, for marriage portions of daughters, and for younger sons' portions to help them establish themselves in a profession or to buy smaller estates of their own. Such provisions were intended to insure that the estate did indeed provide for the family as a whole, while maintaining the integrity of the basic estate as a viable, vital entity, a core around which the family could define itself through many generations.

That there is a breakdown in provision for Mrs. Bennet and her daughters after Mr. Bennet's death is directly linked to the fact that the inheritance of the Bennet estate is determined by strict settlement, the "entailment" that Mrs. Bennet rails against so vehemently in the novel. But the existence of the entailment, though contributing to the problem, is not the full cause of it.

Reading the novel nearly two hundred years after it was written, we generally accept the book's insistence that it is the nature of the entail to be unbreakable, and we interpret Mrs. Bennet's rage against it as part of her general silliness. But in fact, Austen's emphasis on the significance of the entail in the lives of the Bennet women can be read in a much more complicated way, as Austen's contemporaries would have been well aware. Had Mr. Bennet used sufficient foresight, he might well at an earlier time in his life have been able to break an entail of the kind placed on the Longbourn estate, thereby managing to provide for his wife and daughters. Even if he had not succeeded in breaking the entail, however, he could have made other provisions for his daughters. But by the time the novel opens, it is too late for Mr. Bennet to provide for his daughters in any way except by their marriage to prosperous men. At this point in the story the entail is indeed unbreakable, and saving sufficient money to provide for their futures is impractical, if not impossible.

Mrs. Bennet accuses her husband of neglecting his duty to provide for his daughters: " 'I do think it is the hardest thing in the world, that your estate should be entailed away from your own children; and I am sure if I had been you, I should have tried long ago to do something or other about it' " (54). From what we know of Mrs. Bennet we can safely assume that, in reality, she would not " 'have tried long ago to do something or other' " about the entail even if she had had the power; she is too caught up in her own luxuries and in the concerns of the moment to have paid close attention to the entail "long ago." But her point is, nonetheless, significant. The time to "do something or other" was well in the past by the time the action of the novel takes place. Mr. Bennet might, however, have been able to have broken the entail by joining with his father in a legal process called "common recovery" earlier in his life.

Common recovery of an estate involves what is essentially a fictitious lawsuit that enables the present tenant (legally the "life tenant") and the heir (legally the "tenant in tail") of the property to join together to break the entailment in order to resettle the property in a manner more fitting to the present conditions of the estate and family. Such actions were usually taken either at the time the heir came of age (twenty-one) or at the time of the heir's marriage settlement. Mr. Bennet may, therefore, have had the opportunity to cooperate with his father in a common recovery suit on Longbourn, then the estate of which his father was life tenant and himself tenant in tail. With sufficient forethought, they could have revised the settlement in such a way as to adequately provide for Mr. Bennet's heirs of *both* genders, either through making the entail general (which would enable the daughters to inherit—a legally appropriate move, though not a conventional one) or through providing in the new settlement greater financial security for daughters in the event that Mr. and Mrs. Bennet did not produce the expected son. Instead, if the Bennet men had the opportunity to resettle the estate (and not all generations in a family did), they clearly did not consider the possibility of exclusively female children and did not revise the settlement adequately to provide for that contingency.

It must be noted, however, that Mr. Bennet is not solely—or even mostly—at fault in the inadequate structure of this settlement. If the property was resettled as a part of the Bennets' marriage settlement, the two fathers would have been likely to have determined most of the provisions. The younger Bennet would have had to agree to them in order for them to be put into effect, but he would have been likely to defer to the authority of his father, especially if, like his father, he had never considered the possibility of failing to sire a male heir.

Mr. Bennet recognizes his negligence late in the novel. Austen writes:

> Mr. Bennet had very often wished . . . that, instead of spending his whole income, he had laid by an annual sum, for the better provision of his children, and of his wife, if she survived him. . . . When first Mr. Bennet had married, economy was held to be perfectly useless; for, of course, they were to have a son. This son was to join in cutting off the entail, as soon as he should be of age, and the widow and younger children would by that means be provided for. Five daughters successively entered the world, but yet the son was to come. . . . This event had at last been despaired of, but it was then too late to be saving. (272)

Without a son to join him in a common recovery of the estate, Mr. Bennet's options were significantly limited. Saving money out of his annual income would have been the logical alternative, but, as Austen suggests, by the time Mr. Bennet recognized the problem, "it was . . . too late to be saving." Mr. Bennet's negligence has created a situation of potential poverty for his wife and five daughters after his death.

Fortunately for the Bennet daughters, major disaster is averted. But in the elopement of Lydia and Wickham, Austen depicts the very real possibility of disaster for a woman of the gentry with little or no fortune. Her father's financial impotence in the situation is the direct result of his financially irresponsible behavior in setting aside no money for his daughters, thus putting their futures in danger and having to rely on others to provide for them.

BRODRICK ON PRIMOGENITURE

In 1881 George C. Brodrick published *English Land and English Landlords*, an in-depth examination of England's property law system of the Victorian period, its application over six centuries, its advantages, and its disadvantages. Brodrick was one of many late Victorian writers who participated in a movement for land law reform, and his discussion of the prevailing system of property law is among the clearest and most thorough published in that period.

The following excerpt is taken from Brodrick's discussion of the law and custom of primogeniture as it had been practiced in England for centuries. He discusses the ways in which entailment (the custom, as opposed to the law, of primogeniture) has been dominant among landed Britishers for two centuries; how the custom of entailment enriches eldest sons while sacrificing their siblings; how landed gentlemen rarely provide fairly, or even adequately at times, for their other children; and how the unquestioned acceptance of the eldest son's *right* to succeed to his family's estate and the bulk of its fortune often creates future heirs who are frivolous and engaged in a constant search for amusement rather than young men intent on learning to rule their estates and guide their families effectively. Darcy is not a frivolous eldest son and heir, but Austen frequently writes of such characters, most notably in *Northanger Abbey, Sense and Sensibility*, and *Mansfield Park*.

As is clear from Brodrick's text promoting land law reform, he believed that both the law and the custom of primogeniture were counterproductive in British society, that in fact primogeniture should be considered the very heart of the land law in need of reform.

FROM GEORGE C. BRODRICK,
ENGLISH LAND AND ENGLISH LANDLORDS:
AN ENQUIRY INTO THE ORIGIN AND CHARACTER OF THE
ENGLISH LAND SYSTEM,
WITH PROPOSALS FOR ITS REFORM
(London: Petter, Galpin and Co., 1881)

The most distinctive features of the English Land-system, as it now exists, are the Law and Custom of Primogeniture governing the ownership of land; the peculiar character of family settlements, which convert the nominal owner of land into a tenant-for-life, with very limited power over the estate; [and] the consequent distribution of landed property and territorial influence among a comparatively small and constantly decreasing number of families. . . .

The Law of Primogeniture, in its strictest form, has now determined the descent of land on intestacy [dying without a will] in this country for more than six centuries. It has been shown that not long after the Norman Conquest the right of an eldest son to inherit his father's estate, if held by knight service, was fully recognised, and had been extended by the end of the thirteenth century. . . . It has also been shown how this right has survived all recent attempts to abolish it, so that, while all personalty [personal property] is divided on the death of his widow and children, all realty [landed property] still devolves, by common law, on the eldest male descendant of the eldest line. The Custom of Primogeniture, under which landed property is usually settled by deed or will upon the eldest male descendant of the eldest line, is of less ancient origin . . . but has prevailed with little variation for the last two centuries. . . .

By the great majority of [the landed aristocracy and those wanting to enter its ranks], embracing the whole nobility, the squires of England, the lairds of Scotland, and the Irish gentry of every degree, Primogeniture is accepted almost as a fundamental law of nature, to which the practice of entails only gives a convenient and effectual expression. Adam Smith [a renowned eighteenth-century economist] remarks that "in Scotland more than one-fifth, perhaps more than one-third, part of the whole lands of the country are at present supposed to be under strict entail." . . . Mr. McCulloch, writing in 1847, calculated that at least half Scotland was then entailed. . . . In England, where so much land is in the hands of corporations or trustees for public objects, and where almost all deeds relating to land are in private custody, we cannot venture to speak with so much confidence on this point. Considering, however, that in most counties large estates predominate over small, and that large estates, by the general testimony of the legal profession, are almost always entailed either by will or settlement, while small estates, if hereditary, are very often entailed, there is no rashness in concluding . . . that a much larger area is under settlement than at the free disposal of individual landlords.

It is well known that in families which maintain the practice of entailing, the disparity of fortune between the eldest son and younger children is almost invariably prodigious. The charge of the portions of the younger children, when created by a marriage settlement, is created at a time when it is quite uncertain how many such children there will be. It is rarely double of the annual rental, and often does not exceed the annual rental; indeed, in the case of very large estates, it may fall very far short of it. In other words, supposing there to be six children, the income of each younger brother or sister from a family property of £5,000 a year will consist of the interest on a sum of £1,000, or, at the utmost, of £2,000; and, even if there were but one such younger child, his income from the property would probably not be more than one-twentieth or one-thirtieth of his elder brother's rental. Nor does this represent the whole difference between their respective shares of the family endowment; for the eldest son, who pays no probate duty, finds a residence and garden at his disposal, which he may either occupy rent-free or let for his own private advantage. Of course, where a father possesses a large amount of personalty, he may partially redress the balance; and there are exceptionally conscientious landowners who feel it a duty to save out of their own life incomes for younger children. But it is to be feared that [such savings] are too often employed, not exclusively nor mainly to increase the pittances allotted for portions, but on the principle of "To him that hath shall be given," to relieve the eldest son in conforming to a conventional standard of dignity.

It is, indeed, wholly delusive to contrast the Law with the Custom of Primogeniture, as if the harsh operation of the former were habitually mitigated by the latter. The contrary tendency is assuredly far more prevalent in the higher ranks of the landed aristocracy; and the younger members of families in this class would generally have reason to congratulate themselves if the law alone were allowed free scope, instead of being aggravated by the effects of the custom. For instance, in the case last supposed, if a family estate of £5,000 a year were charged with no portions for younger children, but left to descend under the law of intestate succession, each of five younger children would lose £1,000, or, at the utmost, £2,000. But then, if the last owner were possessed of £90,000 in personalty, and this also were left to be divided among the children under the Statute of Distributions, each child would receive a share of £15,000. Suppose, however,—and it is no improbable supposition—that portions have been charged for younger children, but that one-third of the personalty, or £30,000, is bequeathed to the head of the family to keep up the place, the fortune of each younger child will be reduced to £12,000, so that he would lose £3,000, and would gain no more than £1,000 or £2,000. But it is not very often that a landowner with a rental of £5,000 a year has £90,000 to leave among his children. The same imaginary obligation to preserve that degree of state and luxury which is expected of country gentlemen with a certain status and acreage offers an obstacle to saving which the majority find insuperable. Besides, nine out of ten men who inherit their estates burdened with charges for their father's widow and younger children would think it Quixotic to lay by out of their available income, as men of business would do, for the benefit of their own children. Hence the proverbial slenderness of a younger son's fortune in families which have a "place," and especially in those which have a title, to be kept up. As for the daughters, their rank is apt to be reckoned as a substantive part of their fortunes; and not only are their marriage portions smaller than would be considered proper in families of equal affluence in the mercantile class, but it is not unfrequently provided that, unless they have children, their property shall ultimately revert to their eldest brother. . . .

It is too often forgotten that Primogeniture, as secured by modern settlements, compels many a territorial family to support, not one "drone" only, but two, with separate establishments yielding no agricultural return. The head of the family, however, is usually a man of mature age, and, feeling the weight of actual responsibility, may well be impelled by the salutary influence of public opinion, as well as by the dictates of his own good conscience, to set a good example. But can this be said with equal truth of the eldest son, upon whom no such responsibility is cast, whose right to succeed is indefeasible, for whom a present income has been reserved out of the rental upon resettlement, and whose power of raising money upon his expectations is unlimited? It is contended, indeed, that an heir born to a great position, and trained from his earliest years to make himself worthy of it, will acquire habits and will be fortified by motives which are powerful securities for his future virtue and capacity. No doubt it may be so, and it would be easy to cite instances of landowners, especially in the higher ranks of the nobility, who devoted themselves in youth to laborious preparation for territorial duties, as others do to a lucrative profession. These instances must be duly taken into account, nor must it be lightly assumed that the choicest results of English Primogeniture could be produced under an opposite system. But are these instances common enough to be treated as typical? Would it be difficult to cite a larger number of instances where the heirs of ancestral estates have been spoiled and demoralized by their great expectations, even if they are afterwards reformed by the effect of realizing these expectations? Would not the senseless frivolities and reckless extravagance of the London season, the scandals of turf speculation, the restless passion for amusement, and the ignoble race of social competition, be sensibly checked by the withdrawal of this *jeunesse dorée* from English society, and especially from those circles in which match-making is the supreme end of human ambition? Would the army be less efficient if it should lose the services of a few officers in the Household Brigade and cavalry regiments, who take up with military life as a gentlemanlike pastime, and have no intention of continuing it for more than a few years? Would the wisdom of Parliament be diminished if the number of young country members were lessened by the subtraction of those who owe their seats to mere acreage and family names? These are questions which cannot be answered by reference to statistics, but on which a knowledge of the world may throw some light, and which must be faced by those who imagine that Primogeniture is maintained at the cost of younger sons alone, and not also at the cost of the country. It may be too much to assert that family settlements induce unprincipled or careless landowners to neglect the education of their eldest sons, knowing that, however worthless or dissipated they may prove, neither the estate nor the social estimation of the family can be diminished; or that family settlements "*often* set up in influential positions as examples to society men of luxurious and idle habits, depraved tastes, and corrupted morals." But they assuredly guarantee wealth and power to men who may be utterly unworthy of either, yet whose conduct and manners are too apt to become a standard for imitation in their own class, and even in the classes below them. If the general effect of such a provision be indeed as beneficial as it is represented to be, we must suppose the ordinary laws of human nature to be reversed for the purpose of justifying the English Law and Custom of Primogeniture. (89–91, 99–102, 114–116)

PROPERTY LAW AND MARRIAGE

Marriage in eighteenth- and early nineteenth-century England was as much (sometimes more) a matter of property as of love or companionship. Under the law, marriage was then treated, as it continues to be today, as an issue of property. But unlike today, the married couple in Austen's England was treated as a single entity under the law, an entity with only one legal identity. Nineteenth-century British legal historian Basil Edwin Lawrence explains: "By marriage the husband and wife became one person in the eyes of the common law; still, no new *'persona'* was created, the *'persona'* of the wife was considered as completely merged in that of the husband, nearly all her property became his *ipso facto*, and his domicile became hers" (1). Or, in the more concise words of prominent eighteenth-century British legal expert Sir William Blackstone: " 'the husband and wife are one, and the husband is that one' " (quoted in Lawrence Stone's *The Family, Sex and Marriage in England, 1500–1800*, 222). The wife, as a separate legal entity, essentially ceased to exist in regard to property, resulting in the fact that she could only act under *cover* of her husband (in accordance with the law of "coverture"). The result of this law was that a married woman, having no independent legal identity in the eyes of the civil law, could not own property in her own right. All rights to property that she owned outright at the time of her marriage were transferred to her husband, as was all control of property she held in trust for future generations.

BLACKSTONE ON MARRIAGE LAW

Sir William Blackstone was one of the most famous and prominent legal experts in England in the eighteenth century. He was born in 1723, the son of Charles Blackstone, a silk merchant, and Mary Bigg Blackstone, a member of the landed aristocracy. Blackstone was raised and educated, along with his brothers, by his uncle, Dr. Thomas Bigg, a successful surgeon in London. Dr. Bigg provided William with an extensive liberal education, and the latter entered Oxford University at the age of fifteen.

In 1753 Blackstone began to teach law at Oxford, though not as part of the regular curriculum, which at the time covered only Roman law. His series of lectures, entitled "An Analysis of the Laws of England," focused instead on English law. In 1758 Blackstone's courses were incorporated into the regular curriculum at Oxford, and in the 1760s he began producing his *Commentaries*. These four volumes have served as essential documents in the interpretation of British law (and all systems of law based on it, including that of the United States) ever since.

Blackstone wrote extensively on many subjects, including the legal consequences of marriage for both men and women. In order to interpret the marital themes of *Pride and Prejudice* appropriately, one needs a solid understanding of the expectations and legalities involved in marriage in England of the eighteenth century, and nowhere is there a clearer and more accurate description of those expectations and legalities than in *Blackstone's Commentaries*.

Blackstone presents a clear definition of the necessary conditions for a legal marriage in eighteenth-century England. He defines the ages of consent, both with and without parental consent, and describes the few conditions that could void a marriage.

The *Commentaries*, however, do more than define legal marriage. They also describe the consequences of marriage under English law, some of which were favorable to women and unfavorable to men, but most of which were of significantly more benefit to husbands than to wives. Note Blackstone's use of the word "adopted" in the second excerpt below. The language choice is not accidental. Married women were consistently compared with minor children and the insane—both categories of people considered incapable of caring for themselves. To marry a woman was, in one sense, to "adopt" her—or at least to adopt responsibility for all the circumstances of life with which she entered the marriage.

A wife, having no identity under the civil law, had no way of applying to the law directly for redress for injuries she suffered, whether at the hands of her husband or someone else. Blackstone writes, "If the wife be injured in her person or property, she cannot sue for redress without her husband's concurrence, and in his name, as well as her own, neither can she be sued, without her husband be also made a defendant. If, however, the husband has abjured the realm, or is banished, she may sue alone, for then he is dead in law" (Vol. 1, 190). Only a husband's death, in reality or "in law," was sufficient to enable a wife to go to court on her own behalf.

The third excerpt in this section describes the law defining a husband's right to "correct" his wife, once again using language that reminds the reader of a wife's connection with minors, subordinates, and servants. In theory, a woman had the right to ask the courts to intervene if she was mistreated by her husband, but in reality, few women (among them only the wealthiest, who had influential family or friends to help bring the suit) ever successfully defended against a husband's cruelty.

The *Commentaries* also addresses quite specifically the subject of a husband's right to his wife's property. In the section entitled "Title by Marriage," Blackstone details those rights: "The sixth mode of acquiring personal property is by marriage, whereby those chattels [possessions], which belonged formerly to the wife, are, by act of law, vested in the husband, with the same degree of property and the same power, as the wife, when sole [single], had over them." In the same section, he also describes the wife's own right to very limited possessions.

As Blackstone makes abundantly clear, the husband had by far the greater legal power. In fact, in the eighteenth century and the early nineteenth century, that power was probably at its strongest, at least in terms of the complete restriction of married women operating for themselves as legal entities.

FROM SIR WILLIAM BLACKSTONE, *COMMENTARIES ON THE LAWS OF ENGLAND*
(Oxford, 1765)

As the law now stands, no marriage by the temporal law is *ipso facto* void, that is celebrated by a person in orders, in a parish church or public chapel, or elsewhere by special dispensation, in pursuance of banns or license, between single persons, consenting, of sound mind, and of the age of twenty-one years; or of the age of fourteen in males, and twelve in females, with the consent of parents or guardians, or without it in the case of widowhood. And no marriage is voidable after the death of either of the parties, nor during their lives, unless for the canonical impediments of precontract, if that still exists, of consanguinity, of affinity or of corporal imbecility existing before marriage. (Vol. 1, 443)

• • •

By marriage, the husband and wife are one person in law, that is, the legal existence of the woman is suspended during marriage, or at least is incorporated into that of the husband, under whose protection and cover, she performs everything, and is therefore called by French law, a *feme covert*, or under the protection of the husband, her baron or lord, and her condition during marriage is one of coverture. A man cannot grant anything to his wife, or enter into covenant with her, for the grant would be to suppose her separate existence, and to contract with her, would be to contract with himself. Also usually all compacts made between the parties, prior to their union, are voided by their intermarriage. . . .

A husband is bound by law to provide necessaries to his wife, and if she contracts debts for them, he is obliged to pay them, but is not chargeable for aught except necessaries. If, however, she elopes [leaves her husband with another man], and the shopkeeper is apprised of the fact, she cannot bind her husband for necessaries furnished. If a wife be indebted before marriage, her husband is bound afterwards to pay such debt, for he has adopted both her and her circumstances. (Vol. 1, 442)

• • •

If the wife be injured in her person or property, she cannot sue for redress without her husband's concurrence, and in his name, as well as her own, neither can she be sued, without her husband be also made a defendant. If, however, the husband has abjured the realm, or is banished, she may sue alone, for then he is dead in law. (Vol. 3, 242)

• • •

Under the old law, the husband might give his wife moderate correction. For as he is to answer for her misbehavior, the law intrusted him with the power of restraining her by domestic chastisement, as he would punish a child or an apprentice. But this power of correction was confined within reasonable bounds, and he was prohibited from using violence. The civil law gave a man even a larger authority over his wife, permitting him to whip her, if he deemed it necessary. This form of correction was checked in the reign of Charles II, and has not been revived, but the courts of law still permit a husband to restrain his wife of her liberty, in case of any gross misbehavior. (Vol. 1, 444)

• • •

In one instance the wife may acquire a property in some of her husband's goods, which shall remain to her after his death, and not go to his executors. These are called her *paraphernalia*, a term used in the civil law . . . signifying something over and above her dower. In our law it signifies the apparel and ornaments of the wife, suitable to her rank and degree. These she retains at the death of her husband, over her jointure or dower. The husband cannot bequeath by his will such ornaments and jewels of his wife, though perhaps during his life he might have the power to dispose of them. But if she continues in their use until her husband's death, she shall afterwards retain them against all persons, except creditors, where there is a deficiency of assets. (Vol. 3, 466)

ALEXANDER ON MARRIED WOMEN'S RIGHTS

William Alexander, author of *The History of Women from the Earliest Antiquity, to the Present Time*, published in 1779, describes the laws restricting the rights of married women as primarily beneficial to those women as well as society, a view that seems to have been held by most of Austen's contemporaries.

By today's standards, of course, the denial of such rights as freedom of individual movement, making a will, and possession of one's own earned or inherited assets merely because one marries seems absurd to most people in Britain and the United States. But in Austen's time, the treatment of the married woman as "a minor" was well established and accepted without question by most of English society, and the "right" of a husband to compel his wife to live as he chose, even to the extent of forcing her to live virtually imprisoned in some cases, was considered valid, though not necessarily virtuous or kind.

FROM WILLIAM ALEXANDER, *THE HISTORY OF WOMEN FROM THE EARLIEST ANTIQUITY, TO THE PRESENT TIME*
(London, 1779, 2 vols.)

By the laws of this country, the moment a woman enters into the state of matrimony, her political existence is annihilated, or incorporated into that of her husband; but by this little mortification she is no loser, and her apparent loss of consequence is abundantly compensated by a long list of extensive privileges and immunities, which, for the encouragement of matrimony, were, perhaps, contrived to give married women the advantage over those that are single. Of all the privileges which nature has conferred upon us, none are so precious and inestimable as personal liberty. Men of all ranks and conditions, and women who are unmarried, or widows, may be deprived of this for debts contracted by themselves, or by others for whom they have given security; but wives cannot be imprisoned for debt, nor deprived of their personal liberty for any things but crimes; and even such of these as subject the offender only to a pecuniary punishment must be expiated by the husband. No married woman is liable to pay any debt, even though contracted without the knowledge, or against the consent of her husband; and what is still more extraordinary, whatever debts she may have contracted while single, devolve, the moment of her marriage, upon the husband, who, like the scape-goat, is loaded by the priest who performs the ceremony with all the sins and extravagances of his wife. . . .

So long as a wife cohabits with her husband, he is, by the laws of his country, obliged to provide her with food, drink, clothing, and all other necessaries suitable to her rank and his circumstances, even although he received no fortune with her. If he leaves her, or forces her to leave him by ill usage, he is also liable to maintain her in the same manner; but if she runs away from him, and he is willing that she should abide in his house, he is not liable to give her any separate maintenance, nor to pay any of her debts, unless he take her again; in which case he must pay whatever she contracts, whether she behave herself ill or well. . . .

Every married woman is considered as a minor, and cannot do any deed which affects her real or personal property without the consent of her husband, and if she does any such deed, it is not valid, and the husband may claim the property of what she disposed of, as if no such disposal had been made. As a married woman cannot dispose of her property while living, so neither does the law give her that power at her death. In the statute of wills, she is expressly prohibited from devising land, and even from bequeathing goods and chattels without the leave of her husband; because all such goods and chattels are, without any limitation, his sole and absolute property; whether they were such as the wife brought along with her at the marriage, or such as she acquired even by her labour and industry afterward.

The laws of this country not only deny to a married woman the power of making a will, but also dissolve and render of no effect upon her marriage all and every will she may have while single; and even when a single woman who has made her will, marries, and her husband dies, the will which she had made, being invalidated by her marriage, does not recover its validity by the husband's death. . . .

When a husband and wife agree to live separate, and the husband covenants to give her so much a year, if at any time he offers to be reconciled and to take her home, upon her refusal, he shall not any longer be obliged to pay her a separate maintenance. If a legacy be paid to a married woman who lives separate from her husband, the husband may file a bill in chancery to oblige the person who paid it to his wife to pay it again to him with interest. If a wife proves insane, the husband, as her proper guardian, has a right to confine her in his own house, or in a private mad-house; but should the husband not be inclined to release her when her senses return, a court of equity will give her that relief which the husband denies. The power which a husband has over the person of his wife does not seem perfectly settled by the laws of this country; it is nevertheless certain, that she is not to go abroad, nor to leave his house and family, without his approbation; but what coercive methods he may make use of to restrain her from so doing, or whether he may proceed any farther than to admonition and denying her money, seems a point not altogether agreed upon. (323–324, 339–340)

MARRIAGE AND PROPERTY RIGHTS

In their 1898 edition of *The History of English Law Before the Time of Edward I*, Sir Frederick Pollock and Frederic William Maitland look back over several centuries of British law and trace its transformations over time. Pollock and Maitland, like Brodrick, were late Victorian advocates of law reform, and their attitudes clearly indicate their reformative purposes. Their interpretation of the development of the idea of coverture illuminates the legal atmosphere surrounding the concepts of marriage and property in Austen's time more clearly than other texts of the period.

The first excerpt discusses the husband's entitlement to his wife's property under English law from a somewhat different viewpoint than Alexander's. In it, Pollock and Maitland merely reiterate the rules of law that Alexander has delineated, though through a more objective lens.

The second excerpt introduces what Pollock and Maitland believe to be the basis for the idea that a husband and wife become one person under the law, an idea that they believe to have been created as a result of faulty logic and shortsighted legal interpretations by lawyers of previous centuries. It is these misinterpretations of earlier law, they believe, that have created what they consider to be the mistaken impression that married women have no identity under the law.

In the third excerpt Pollock and Maitland present their explanation of how British common law came to treat husband and wife as one entity under the law (and that entity, the husband) instead of treating their holdings in common ("community property"). This change in the way common law was viewed and interpreted by the eighteenth and nineteenth centuries may well account for the fact that in the Middle Ages British women seem to have had much greater control over their own finances than did the women of Austen's time.

As a result of this interpretation of the existing civil legal code, women's rights to property and to their own persons were severely restricted as soon as they married.

In the final excerpt Pollock and Maitland discuss the fact that English law gives husbands more complete control and more secure rights to their wives' property than do the legal systems most closely allied with the English: the Norman, the Scottish, and the Irish systems.

Pollock and Maitland's theory about the development of the "courteous" concept of coverture explains several seeming-contradictions in the history of British property law. But we must remember when reading Austen's novels that people of her time believed, as Blackstone and Alexander expressed so eloquently, that married women had no independent legal identity, that their identities were subsumed into those of their husbands, and that their legal rights, independent of their husbands' will, were slight. While marriage might be the only way for women like the Bennet daughters to establish security, that security would always be dependent on the inclination of the men they married. Thus, the character of the men they choose to marry, and their ability to provide financially for a wife are of the utmost importance in the world of *Pride and Prejudice*, as they were for all women of the gentry who were contemporaries of Jane Austen.

FROM SIR FREDERICK POLLOCK AND FREDERIC WILLIAM
MAITLAND, *THE HISTORY OF ENGLISH LAW BEFORE THE TIME
OF EDWARD I*
(London, 1898, 2nd. ed., 2 vols.)

Our law institutes no community even of movables between husband and wife. Whatever movables the wife has at the date of the marriage, become the husband's, and the husband is entitled to take possession of and thereby to make his own whatever movables she becomes entitled to during the marriage, and without her concurrence he can sue for all debts that are due to her. On his death, however, she becomes entitled to all movables and debts that are outstanding. . . . What the husband gets possession of is simply his; he can freely dispose of it. . . . If she dies in his lifetime, she can have no other intestate successor. Without his consent she can make no will, and any consent he may have given is revocable at any time before the will is proved. . . .

During the marriage the husband is in effect liable to the whole extent of his property for debts incurred or wrongs committed by his wife before the marriage, also for wrongs committed during the marriage. The action is against him and her as co-defendants. If the marriage is dissolved by his death, she is liable, his estate is not. If the marriage is dissolved by her death, he is liable as her administrator, but only to the extent of the property he takes in that character.

During the marriage the wife can not contract on her own behalf. She can contract as her husband's agent, and has a certain power of pledging his credit in the purchase of necessaries. . . . The tendency . . . has been to allow her no power that can not be thus explained, except in the exceptional case of desertion. (404–405)

• • •

[W]e may now turn back to the twelfth and thirteenth centuries. If we look for any one thought which governs the whole of this province of law, we shall hardly find it. In particular we must be on our guard against the common belief that the ruling principle is that which sees an "unity of person" between husband and wife. This is a principle which suggests itself from time to time; it has the warrant of holy writ; it will serve to round a paragraph, and may now and again lead us out of or into a difficulty; but a consistently operative principle it can not be. We do not treat the wife as a thing or as somewhat that is neither thing nor person; we treat her as a person. Thus Bracton tells us that if either the husband without the wife, or the wife without the husband, brings an action for the wife's land, the defendant can take exception to this "for they are *quasi* one person, for they are one flesh and one blood." But this impracticable proposition is followed by a real working principle:—"for the thing is the wife's own and the husband is guardian as being the head of the wife." The husband is the wife's guardian:—that we believe to be the fundamental principle: and it explains a great deal, when we remember that guardianship is a profitable right. . . . [T]he husband's right in the wife's lands can be regarded as an exaggerated guardianship. The wife's subjection to her husband is often insisted on; she is "wholly within his power," she is bound to obey him in all that is not contrary to the law of God; she and all her property ought to be at his disposal; she is "under the rod." (405–406)

• • •

We are not contending that the law of England ever definitely recognized a community of goods between husband and wife. We have, however, seen many rules as to what takes place on the dissolution of the marriage which might easily have been explained as the outcome of such a community, had our temporal lawyers been free to consider and administer them. Unfortunately about the year 1200 they suffered the ecclesiastical courts to drive a wedge into the law of husband and wife which split it in twain. The lay lawyer had thenceforth no immediate concern with what would happen on the dissolution of the marriage [since the ecclesiastical courts made dissolution of marriage impossible, for all practical purposes]. He had merely to look at the state of things that existed during the marriage. Looking at this, he saw only the husband's absolute power to deal with the chattels *inter vivos*. Had he been compelled to meditate upon the fate which would befall this mass of goods so soon as one of the spouses died, he might have come to a conclusion which his foreign brethren accepted, namely, that the existence of a community is by no means disproved by the absolute power of the husband, who is so long as the marriage endures "the head of the community." As it was, he saw only the present, not the future, the present unity of the mass, not its future division into shares. And so he said boldly that the whole mass belonged to the husband. "It is adjudged that the wife has nothing of her own while her husband lives, and can make no purchase with money of her own." "She had and could have no chattel of her own while her husband lived." "Whatsoever is the wife's is the husband's, and the converse is not true." "The wife has no property in chattels during the life of her husband." "This demand supposes that the property in a chattel may be in the wife during the life of her husband, which the law does not allow."

Once more we see the lawyers of the thirteenth century making a short cut. A short cut it is, as all will allow who have glanced at the many difficulties which the idea of a "community" has to meet. When they gave to the husband the ownership of the wife's chattels, they took an important step. Having taken it, they naturally set themselves against the wife's testamentary power [the power to make a will] (for how can Jane have a right to bequeath things that belong to John?) and they set themselves against every restraint of the husband's testamentary power (for why should not a man bequeath things that belong to him?), they secured for the widow nothing but the clothes upon her back. (432–433)

• • •

[T]he right given to the husband by English law is a large, a liberal right. It comprehends the wife's lands by whatever title she may have acquired them, whether by way of inheritance or by way of marriage portion, or by any other way; it endures though there is no longer any issue [child] of the marriage in existence; it endures though the husband has married another wife; it is given to a second husband, who can thereby keep out a son of the first marriage from his inheritance. About these points there has been controversy, but at every point the husband has been victorious. . . .

If we compare our law with its nearest of kin, we see a peculiar favour shown to the husband. Norman law deprives him of his right when he marries again; at any rate he must then give up two-thirds of the land.

Scottish law gives him his "curtesy" only in lands which his wife has inherited, not in lands which have been given to her. The English lawyers know that their law is peculiar, believe that it has its origin in some "specialty." This being so, it is by no means unnatural that they should call it "courteous," or as we might say "liberal" law. They look at the matter from the husband's point of view; this is the popular point of view. (416–417)

TOPICS FOR WRITTEN OR ORAL EXPLORATION

1. Write a paper (or make a class presentation) in which you explain how the entailment of the Longbourn property in *Pride and Prejudice* works.

2. Divide the class into two teams. Then prepare and initiate a debate, one side arguing for the positive effects of the law of primogeniture and the practice of entailment on eighteenth- and nineteenth-century British society, the other arguing for the negative effects of the law and practice on that society.

3. Write an essay on your own family structure and how you would fare personally if the law and practice of primogeniture applied in the United States of the present day. Would the existence of primogeniture change your life? The lives of your siblings? The lives of your parents? How would these lives be changed?

4. When women married in eighteenth- and nineteenth-century England, any property they owned legally became the property of their husbands. How do you think this transfer of property affected relationships between husbands and wives? What would be the advantages of such a system? What would be the disadvantages?

5. Research the marriage laws regarding property in your state. Then write an essay explaining how fair or unfair those property laws are. Be sure to argue your position based on specific evidence.

6. Imagine yourself as an early nineteenth-century English gentlewoman with an estate of your own that could support you comfortably (but not richly) for the rest of your life. Then imagine that you were courted by a very wealthy gentleman who could supply you with a much more luxurious lifestyle if you married him. Would you be willing to marry him, knowing that you would be giving him control of your estate? What issues would you have to consider before agreeing to marry him or refusing his offer?

7. Imagine yourself as an early nineteenth-century English gentleman with a comfortable (but not wealthy) estate. You meet, court, and marry a woman with an estate as large as or larger than yours. You know that you have legal control of both estates and that society expects you to be in control of both. If she wanted to continue controlling the estate that she brought into the marriage, would you allow her to do so? If so, to what extent? If not, why not? How would you handle her displeasure if you refused to give her control? How would you handle public opinion if you allowed her to control openly the

property she brought into the marriage? Supply reasons for your actions.

SUGGESTED READINGS

Alexander, William. *The History of Women from the Earliest Antiquity, to the Present Time*. 2 vols. London: W. Strahan and T. Cadell, 1779.

Blackstone, Sir William. *Commentaries on the Laws of England*. London: John Murray, 1857.

Bonfield, Lloyd. *Marriage Settlements, 1601–1740: The Adoption of the Strict Settlement*. Cambridge: Cambridge University Press, 1983.

Brodrick, George C. *English Land and English Landlords*. London: Petter, Galpin and Co., 1881.

Clay, Christopher. "Marriage, Inheritance, and the Rise of Large Estates in England, 1660–1815." *Economic History Review*, 2nd ser., 21 (1968): 503–18.

Davidoff, Leonore, and Catherine Hall. *Family Fortunes: Men and Women of the English Middle Class, 1780–1850*. Chicago: University of Chicago Press, 1987.

English, Barbara, and John Saville. *Strict Settlement: A Guide for Historians*. Hull, Eng.: University of Hull Press, 1983.

Harding, Alan. *A Social History of English Law*. Harmondsworth: Penguin, 1966.

Hardy, Barbara. "Property and Possessions in Jane Austen's Novels." In *Jane Austen's Achievement*. Edited by Juliet McMaster. London: Macmillan, 1976. 79–105.

Kenny, C. S. *The History of the Law of England as to the Effects of Marriage on Property and on the Wife's Legal Capacity*. London: Reeves and Turner, 1879.

Lawrence, Basil Edwin. *The History of the Laws Affecting the Property of Married Women in England*. London: Reeves and Turner, 1884.

The Laws Respecting Women, as They Regard Their Natural Rights, or Their Connections and Conduct. 4 vols. London: J. Johnson, 1777.

Mingay, G. E. *English Landed Society in the Eighteenth Century*. London: Routledge and Kegan Paul, 1963.

Simpson, A.W.B. *A History of the Land Law*. 2nd ed. Oxford: Clarendon, 1986.

Spring, David. *The English Landed Estate in the Nineteenth Century: Its Administration*. Baltimore: Johns Hopkins University Press, 1963.

Spring, Eileen. *Law, Land, and Family: Aristocratic Inheritance in En-*

gland, 1300–1800. Chapel Hill: University of North Carolina Press, 1993.

Staves, Susan. *Married Women's Separate Property in England, 1660–1883*. Cambridge, MA: Harvard University Press, 1990.

Stone, Lawrence. *The Family, Sex and Marriage in England, 1500–1800*. New York: Harper and Row, 1977.

Stone, Lawrence, and Jeanne C. Fawtier Stone. *An Open Elite? England, 1540–1880*. Oxford: Clarendon, 1984.

Thompson, F.M.L. *English Landed Society in the Nineteenth Century*. London: Routledge and Kegan Paul, 1963.

3

Eighteenth-Century Views of Marriage

The law as it applied to marriage in the eighteenth century was examined in the last chapter, but legality is only one part of the picture. Various and often contradictory ideas about how the institution of marriage was supposed to be lived abounded in the eighteenth century. Many people wrote about proper behavior in marriage—about guidelines for choosing a marriage partner, about what to expect from marriage, about the duties and responsibilities of each spouse, even in a few cases about the unfairness and/or immorality of the institution as it was constituted at that time in history.

It was a time of serious reconsideration of what marriage meant and how it was to be lived. The traditional view of marriage as a joining of families (and family fortunes) through the physical joining of two people continued to have much support. Viewing marriage as a business venture between families, therefore, continued to be widely accepted. At the same time, however, the political and social climate was encouraging the view of the individual *as* an individual. As a result, the preferences of individuals became more important than in the past, and marriage, while still a contract, started to gain acceptance as an affective relationship—one in which the feelings and emotions of the individuals involved were given more consideration than previously. The idea of marrying for love took hold of many in society at this time. As a result, difficult, sometimes disastrous, conflicts often arose, as some family members, often of the older generations, maintained the concept that marriage was primarily a business contract, whereas others supported the newer concept of marriage as a joining of individuals in love.

The first two documents included in this chapter were written early in the eighteenth century by famous British essayists, Samuel Johnson and Daniel Defoe. Johnson's essay from *The Rambler* discusses marriage as a general state, and concludes that marriage is no more unhappy, generally speaking, than is life. Johnson's view is that marriage is a necessary part of life and that people should approach it as such and make the best of it. Defoe, however, detested marriage as it was currently practiced, branding it, in essence, a legalized form of prostitution. Only if love is the foundation of the marital relationship, insists Defoe, can it be meaningful and valid in the eyes of God.

John Gregory, Lady Sarah Pennington, and Thomas Gisborne do not focus on the function of marriage in society; instead they advise about the proper ways to engage in that all-consuming project of most young women of the day—finding and marrying an appropriate husband. The advice the three writers offer differs to some extent in specifics, but all insist on a young lady's need for ultimate propriety, respectability, and common sense if she is to attract a husband who can both provide for her and treat her respectfully. Love, for all three, enters the discussion rather late—only after the issues of physical security and social respectability are addressed.

At the end of the eighteenth century, William Godwin and Mary Wollstonecraft focused attention on the ways in which marriage as it was practiced at the time was cruel and inhumane. Both writers believed that divorce should be much more accessible in the case of impossible marriages, and questioned whether the concept of marriage itself was outdated and irrelevant to personal happiness. Their writings, while much too extreme to garner much direct support, did, in fact, help to create a climate in which marriage law and custom were debated publicly, especially in terms of the rights of women and children. Although the law regarding marriage and custody was very slow to change, the writings of Godwin, Woll-stonecraft, and others who shared their views began an important movement toward greater rights for married women and their children that did not come to full fruition until the twentieth century.

MARRIAGE AS AN INSTITUTION

SAMUEL JOHNSON

Number 45 of *The Rambler* appeared in the year 1750. In it Samuel Johnson addresses the subject of marriage generally. He posits that "marriage is not commonly unhappy, otherwise than as life is unhappy," and proceeds to discuss what he considers to be the positive and negative aspects of the institution as it is customarily practiced. His essay addresses many of the issues people were concerned about, including putting financial considerations above personal compatibility, and preventing one's intended from seeing one's true self until after the marriage ceremony has been performed and no return is legally allowable.

Johnson clearly believed that, in general, marriage added to a person's happiness, but he saw the original motivations for the match and the customary rituals of courting as the source of much incompatability between spouses. For him, the traditional reasons for marriage (business connections for families, etc.) were not wrong in and of themselves, but attention *only* to business at the expense of any consideration of the long-term needs and desires of the individuals involved was immoral and caused much unneeded pain.

FROM SAMUEL JOHNSON, *THE RAMBLER*
(Number 45, August 21, 1750)

I believe . . . that marriage is not commonly unhappy, otherwise than as life is unhappy; and that most of those who complain of connubial miseries, have as much satisfaction as their nature would have admitted, or their conduct procured, in any other condition. . . .

Wives and husbands are, indeed, incessantly complaining of each other; and there would be reason for imagining that every house was infested with perverseness or oppression beyond human sufferance, did we not know upon how small occasions some minds burst out into lamentations and reproaches, and how naturally every animal revenges his pain upon those who happen to be near, without any nice examination of its cause. . . .

When I see the avaricious and the crafty taking companions to their tables, and their beds, without any inquiry, but after farms and money; or the giddy and thoughtless uniting themselves for life to those whom they have only seen by the light of tapers at a ball; when parents make articles for their children without inquiring after their consent; when some marry for heirs to disappoint their brothers, and others throw themselves into the arms of those whom they do not love, because they have found themselves rejected where they were most solicitous to please: when some marry because their servants cheat them, some because they squander their own money, some because their houses are pestered with company, some because they will live like other people, and some only because they are sick of themselves, I am not so much inclined to wonder that marriage is sometimes unhappy, as that it appears so little loaded with calamity; and cannot but conclude that society has something in itself eminently agreeable to human nature, when I find its pleasures so great, that even the ill choice of a companion can hardly overbalance them.

By the ancient custom of the Muscovites, the men and women never saw each other till they were joined beyond the power of parting. It may be suspected that by this method many unsuitable matches were produced, and many tempers associated that were not qualified to give pleasure to each other. Yet, perhaps, among a people so little delicate, where the paucity of gratifications, and the uniformity of life, gave no opportunity of or imagination to interpose its objects, there was not much danger of capricious dislike; and while they felt neither cold nor hunger, they might live quietly together, without any thought of the defects of one another.

Amongst us, whom knowledge has made nice, and affluence wanton, there are, indeed, more cautions requisite to secure tranquillity; and yet if we observe the manner in which those converse, who have singled out each other for marriage, we shall, perhaps, not think that the Russians lost much by their restraint. For the whole endeavour of both parties, during the time of courtship, is to hinder themselves from being known, and to disguise their natural temper, and real desires, in hypocritical imitation, studied compliance, and continual affectation. From the time that their love is avowed, neither sees the other but in a mask, and the cheat is managed often on both sides with so much art, and discovered afterwards with so much abruptness, that each has reason to suspect that some transformation has happened on the wedding night, and that, by a strange imposture, one has been courted, and another married. (243–247)

DANIEL DEFOE

Daniel Defoe, most famous for his novels *Robinson Crusoe* and *Moll Flanders*, wrote the essay *Conjugal Lewdness* in 1727. In it he sets forth what he perceives to be the purpose of marriage and the proper ways of achieving it. His Puritan background is evident in his depiction of sexual pleasure as sinful lust, even in marriage. A marriage based on lust, for the Puritans, was not a blessed union in the eyes of God. Instead, sex in marriage was to be engaged in only for higher purposes, such as the bringing forth of new lives to be dedicated to God.

Like Johnson, Defoe argues against marrying from financial motivation, though his argument is based more on religious and moral precepts than on the kind of reasoned practicality Johnson presents in his essay. For Defoe, marriage for any other reason than love—a love based in sound Puritan theology—was wrong, was, in his words "hardly lawful . . . not rational, and . . . can never be happy."

Few authors would go as far as Defoe in condemning marriages based on financial considerations or motivated by lust as equivalent to prostitution, but the issue of marital motivation was one of great contention in the eighteenth century and the early nineteenth century. Much of the imaginative literature of the day (especially novels) promoted the idea of marrying for love, with or without financial consideration or parental approval. Most of the conduct books of the age, however, emphasized the importance of prudence and of attention to parental concern in one's choice (or refusal) of a mate.

FROM DANIEL DEFOE, *CONJUGAL LEWDNESS*
(London, 1727)

The great duty between the man and his wife, I take to consist in that of love, in the government of affection, and the obedience of a complaisant, kind, obliging temper: the obligation is reciprocal, 'tis drawing in an equal yoke. Love knows no superior or inferior, no imperious command on one hand, no reluctant subjection on the other; the end of both should be the well-ordering of their family, the good-guiding their household and children, educating, instructing and managing them with mutual endeavour. . . .

Ask the ladies why they marry, they tell you 'tis for a good settlement; tho' they had their own fortunes to settle on themselves before. Ask the men why they marry, it is for money. How few matches have any other motive. . . . How little is regarded of that one essential and absolutely necessary part of the composition, called love, without which the matrimonial state is, I think, hardly lawful, I am sure is not rational, and, I think, can never be happy. (26–28)

• • •

In their permission and licence, they must be sure to observe the order of Nature, and the ends of God. He is an ill husband, that uses his wife as a man treats a harlot, having no other end but pleasure. Concerning which our best rule is, that although in this, as in eating and drinking, there is an appetite to be satisfied, which cannot be done without pleasing that desire; yet since that desire and satisfaction was intended by nature for other ends, they should never be separate from those ends, with a desire of children, or to avoid fornication, or to lighten and ease the cares and sadnesses of household affairs, or to endear each other; but never with a purpose, either in act or desire to separate the sensuality from these ends which hallow it. (54–55)

• • •

Will you live with a man, and lie with a man you don't love? . . . 'tis but a kind of legal prostitution, in the plain English of it, too gross and wicked to express. We must not say she is a whore, because the law makes it a literal contract and marriage. But God forbid I should ever say 'twill pass for matrimony in heaven; the young lady in short, is willing . . . to lie with a man; and she takes a fellow that is just in the same condition, under the influence of some lewd appetite, and he desires to lie with a woman. They are both willing to gratify their vicious part in the formality of a legal appointment, and so they agree to marry in form, and they are called man and wife; as such she throws off the mask of modesty, goes into the naked bed to him, or suffers him to come to bed to her; and as they came together upon the mere principles of desire, as above, so they act the several excesses and all the conjugal madnesses, chamberings and wantonnesses . . . and all the while not one ounce of affection, not a grain of original, chaste, and rivetted love . . . is to be found between them.

Is this matrimony! . . . Forbid it, O heaven! that I should call it by that honourable and religious title: On the contrary, it merits . . . nothing less or more than the title of matrimonial whoredom, or, at least of a matrimonial prostitution. (105–106)

HOW TO CHOOSE A HUSBAND

JOHN GREGORY

Conduct books were extremely popular in the late eighteenth century and the early nineteenth century. Most were specifically addressed to young women, and some were even printed in a size small enough to fit in a pocket or small handbag, so that readers could conveniently consult them wherever they might find the time. Most conduct books for young women addressed the subject of marriage explicitly. Some, like the one Mr. Collins reads to the Bennet girls, were in the form of sermons that instructed young women about proper behavior in social as well as religious situations. John Gregory, a physician and philosopher as well as the father of daughters, wrote *A Father's Legacy to His Daughters*, first published in 1774. For almost fifty years it remained one of the most popular and influential essays on proper behavior and education for young women.

His treatise gives advice on many subjects, including that of choosing a husband. Unlike Johnson and Defoe, Gregory does not make ethical and moral judgments about what a woman should look for in a mate, but he does warn them of many possible problems they could encounter if they marry the wrong man. In his own words: "I could never pretend to advise whom you should marry: but I can with great confidence advise whom you should *not* marry."

Like most writers of conduct books in the period, Gregory warns women not to give their hearts too easily and not to mistake mere attraction for abiding love. In fact, he asserts that "without any unusual share of natural sensibility, and very peculiar good fortune, a woman in this country has very little probability of marrying for love." He advises his daughters to base their choice of a husband on character and ability to provide for a wife rather than on such a transitory emotion as romantic love. "Genuine love," as he defines it, may grow from virtue, honor, similar tastes, and sympathetic love; the emotion of romantic love, "passion," can never be as secure.

Among Gregory's most controversial pieces of advice is never to let one's husband know how much one loves him, if indeed one does. This advice is not original, of course, but Gregory's frankness of expression offended many people of his day, both men and women. In the second excerpt, Gregory advises his daughters about choosing their attachments wisely and learning to love prudently and modestly, even if doing so requires being false about the extent of their emotional involvement with their spouses. Note the emphasis on love growing from the roots of "gratitude," especially "if it meets with crosses and difficulties." In *Pride and Prejudice* Elizabeth notes her own gratitude to Darcy as a primary factor in her growing attachment to him. Unlike Gregory's essay, Austen's novel does not advocate falsehood between partners, but it does recognize many of the same motivating factors for marriage.

Gregory's view of happiness in marriage, for women at least, is clearly based on the concept of marriage as a joining of compatible individuals. Regardless of the fortune, prestige, or physical attractiveness of the men courting them, women should, according to Gregory, take long-term compatibility into account. In addition, a woman should always, even after marriage, keep a man guessing about the degree of feeling she has for him. Anything less could make her husband lose respect for her.

FROM JOHN GREGORY, *A FATHER'S LEGACY TO HIS DAUGHTERS* (1774)

Whatever your views are in marrying, take every possible precaution to prevent their being disappointed. If fortune, and the pleasures it brings, are your aim, it is not sufficient that the settlements of a jointure and children's provisions be ample, and properly secured; it is necessary that you should enjoy the fortune during your own life. The principal security you can have for this will depend on your marrying a good-natured, generous man, who despises money, and who will let you live where you can best enjoy that pleasure, that pomp and parade of life, for which you married him. . . .

Avoid a companion that may entail any hereditary disease on your posterity; particularly (that most dreadful of all human calamities) madness. It is the height of imprudence to run into such a danger, and in my opinion, hugely criminal.

Do not marry a fool; he is the most intractable of all animals: he is led by his passions and caprices, and is incapable of hearing the voice of reason. It may probably, too, hurt your vanity to have husbands, for whom you have reason to blush and tremble every time they open their lips in company. But the worst circumstance that attends a fool, is his constant jealousy of his wife being thought to govern him. This renders it impossible to lead him, and he is continually doing absurd and disagreeable things, for no other reason but to shew he dares do them.

A rake is always a suspicious husband, because he has only known the most worthless of your sex. He likewise entails the worst diseases on his wife and children, if he has the misfortune to have any.

If you have a sense of religion yourselves, do not think of husbands who have none. If they have tolerable understandings they will be glad that you have religion, for their own sakes, and for the sake of their families; but it will sink you in their esteem. If they are weak men, they will be continually teazing and shocking you about your principles. If you have children, you will suffer the most bitter distress, in seeing all your endeavours to form their minds to virtue and piety, all your endeavours to secure their present and eternal happiness, frustrated, and turned into ridicule.

As I look on your choice of a husband to be of the greatest consequence to your happiness, I hope you will make it with the utmost circumspection. Do not give way to a sudden sally of passion, and dignify it with the name of love. Genuine love is not founded in caprice; it is founded in nature, on honourable views, on virtue, on similarity of tastes, and sympathy of souls. (185–186)

• • •

People whose sentiments, and particularly whose tastes, correspond, naturally like to associate together, although neither of them have the most distant view of any farther connexion. But, as this similarity of minds often gives rise to a more tender attachment than friendship, it will be prudent to keep a watchful eye over yourselves, lest your hearts become too far engaged before you are aware of it. At the same time, I do not think that your sex, at least in this part of the world, have much of that sensibility which disposes to such attachment. What is commonly called love among you, is rather gratitude, and a partiality to the man who prefers you to the rest of your sex: and such a man you often marry, with little of either personal esteem or affection. Indeed, without any unusual share of natural sensibility, and very peculiar good fortune, a woman in this country has very little probability of marrying for love.

It is a maxim laid down among you, and a very prudent one it is, that love is not to begin on your part, but is entirely to be the consequence of our attachment to you. Now, supposing a woman to have sense and taste, she will not find many men to whom she can possibly be supposed to bear any considerable share of esteem. Among these few, it is very great chance if any of them distinguishes her particularly. Love, at least with us, is exceedingly capricious, and will not always fix where reason says it should. But, supposing one of them should become particularly attached to her, it is still extremely improbable that he should be the man in the world her heart most approved of.

As, therefore, nature has not given you that unlimited range in your choice which we enjoy, she has wisely and benevolently assigned to you a greater flexibility of taste on this subject. Some agreeable qualities recommend a gentleman to your common liking and friendship. In the course of his acquaintance, he contracts an attachment to you. When you perceive it, it excites your gratitude; this gratitude rises into preference; and this preference, perhaps, at last advances to some degree of attachment, especially if it meets with crosses and difficulties: for these, and a state of suspense, are very great incitements to attachment, and are the food of love in both sexes. If attachment was not excited in your sex in this manner, there is not one of a million of you that could ever marry with any degree of love.

A man of taste and delicacy marries a woman because he loves her more than any other; a woman of equal taste and delicacy marries him, because she esteems him, and because he gives her his preference. . . .

A man of delicacy often betrays his passion by his too great anxiety to conceal it, especially if he has little hopes of success. True love, in all its states, seeks concealment, and never expects success; it renders a man not only respectful, but timid to the highest degree in his behaviour to the woman he loves. To conceal the awe he stands in of her, he may sometimes affect pleasantry, but it sits awkwardly on him, and he quickly relapses into seriousness, if not into dulness. He magnifies all her real perfections in his imagination, and is either blind to her failings, or converts them into beauties. Like a person conscious of guilt, he is jealous that every eye observes him; and, to avoid this, he shuns all the little observances of common gallantry.

His heart and his character will be improved in every respect by his attachment; his manners will become more gentle, and his conversation more agreeable; but diffidence and embarrassment will always make him appear to disadvantage in the company of his mistress. If the fascination continue long, it will totally depress his spirit, and extinguish every active, vigorous, and manly principle of his mind. . . .

When you observe in a gentleman's behaviour, these marks which I have described above, reflect seriously what you are to do. If his attachment is agreeable to you, I leave you to do as Nature, good sense, and delicacy shall direct you. If you love him, let me advise you never to discover to him the full extent of your love; no, not although you marry him. *That* sufficiently shews your preference, which is all he is entitled to know. If he has delicacy, he will ask for no strong proof of your affection for *your* sake; if he has sense, he will not ask it for *his own*. This is an unpleasant truth; but it is my duty to let you know it. Violent love cannot subsist, at least cannot be expressed, for any time together, on both sides; otherwise the certain consequence, however concealed, is satiety and disgust. Nature, in this case, has laid the reserve on you. . . .

A woman, in this country, may easily prevent the first impressions of love; and every motive of prudence and delicacy should make her guard her heart against them, till such time as she has received the most convincing proofs of the attachment of a man of such merit, as will justify a reciprocal regard. Your hearts indeed may be shut inflexibly and permanently against all the merits a man can possess. That may be your misfortune, but cannot be your fault. In such a situation, you would be equally unjust to yourself and your lover, if you give him your hand when your heart revolted against him. But miserable will be your fate, if you allow an attachment to steal on you before you are aware of a return: or, what is infinitely worse, where there are wanting those qualities which alone can ensure happiness in a married state.

I know nothing that renders a woman more despicable, than her thinking it essential to happiness to be married. Besides the gross indelicacy of the sentiment, it is a false one, as thousands of women have experience. But if it was true, the belief that it is so, and the consequent impatience to be married, is the most effectual way to prevent it.

You must not think from this, that I do not wish you to marry: on the contrary, I am of opinion, that you may attain a superior degree of happiness in a married state, to what you can possibly find in any other. I know the forlorn and unprotected situation of an old maid, the chagrin and peevishness which are apt to infect their tempers, and the great difficulty of making a transition with dignity and cheerfulness, from the period of youth, beauty, admiration, and respect, into the calm, silent, unnoticed retreat of declining years. . . .

I am of opinion, that a married state, if entered into from proper motives of esteem and affection, will be the happiest for yourselves, make you most respectable in the eyes of the world, and the most useful members of society. But I confess, I am not enough of a patriot to wish you to marry for the good of the public: I wish you to marry for no other reason but to make yourselves happier. When I am so particular in my advices about your conduct, I own my heart beats with the fond hope of making you worthy [of] the attachment of men who will deserve you, and be sensible of your merit. But Heaven forbid you should ever relinquish the ease and independence of a single life, to become the slaves of a fool or a tyrant's caprice. (172–175, 177–181)

Source: Hester Chapone, Dr. John Gregory, and Lady Pennington, *Chapone's Improvement of the Mind; Gregory's Legacy; Lady Pennington's Advice* (London: Scott and Webster, n.d.).

LADY SARAH PENNINGTON

Lady Sarah Pennington, like Dr. Gregory, addresses her book of advice to her daughters, but whereas Gregory's daughters were living with him at the time he wrote his treatise, Lady Pennington's daughters were taken from her by her husband, a man who used, abused, and separated from her. Under eighteenth-century British law, a mother had no rights to her children, only whatever privileges their father allowed her. Sir Joseph Pennington forbade Lady Pennington to have any contact with her daughters after their separation.

Subsequently, she wrote and published *An Unfortunate Mother's Advice to Her Absent Daughters*, a conduct manual that she hoped her daughters would benefit from reading. She addresses the work to her eldest daughter, Jenny, and begins with an explanation of her choice of so public a forum for what she would have preferred to have been much more private advice:

> My Dear Jenny,
>   Was there any probability that a letter from me would be permitted reach your hand alone, I would not have chosen this least eligible method of writing to you.—The public is no way concerned in family affairs, and ought not to be made a party in them;—but my circumstances are such as lay me under a necessity of either communicating my sentiments to the world, or of concealing them from you;—the latter would, I think, be the breach of an indispensable duty, which obliges me to waive the impropriety of the former. (191)

Lady Pennington thus explains that this public display, something not considered appropriate for ladies of the day, is made necessary by circumstances. Moreover, her interest in warning her daughters about the dangers of bad marriages is strongly influenced by her own experience. Having married without her family's express approval, she chose a man who mistreated her. She warns her daughters not to make the same kinds of mistakes that she made. Like

Gregory and most authors of conduct books of the day, Lady Pennington warns her daughters about the dangers of marrying where one cannot "esteem."

Note particularly the distinction Lady Pennington makes in the following excerpt between a man who is ill-natured and one who is merely ill-humored. This distinction is particularly appropriate to the study of Mr. Darcy and Mr. Wickham in *Pride and Prejudice*. Lady Pennington's advice on how to tell the one quality from the other can be used to distinguish Darcy's true character from that of Wickham, and her advice might have served Elizabeth well early in the novel by "effectually secur[ing her] from the dangerous error of taking the shadow for the substance—an irretrievable mistake, pregnant with innumerable consequent evils" (223).

Jane Austen might almost be writing parts of *Pride and Prejudice* with Lady Pennington's advice in mind. Elizabeth judges Darcy first on his ill humor in company—at a ball where he is uncomfortable and knows few people—and first judges Wickham by his correspondingly good humor (not seeing his ill nature until late in the novel). The time at which Elizabeth seems to come to a true understanding of Darcy is when she visits Pemberley with her aunt and uncle. The good character that the housekeeper and tenants of Darcy's estate give of him finally convinces Elizabeth that her preliminary judgment, her "prejudice," was wrong. She had judged Darcy before she had sufficient information; she had judged him on his appearance in company rather than on his essential self—the domestic self, at home with his servants, his tenants, and his private duties. If Elizabeth had known and considered Lady Pennington's advice prior to meeting Darcy and Wickham, she might have been less critical of the former and less entranced by the latter early in the game.

FROM LADY SARAH PENNINGTON, *AN UNFORTUNATE MOTHER'S ADVICE TO HER ABSENT DAUGHTERS*
(1761)

Happy is her lot, who, in a husband, finds this invaluable friend! yet, so great is the hazard, so disproportioned the chances, that I could almost wish the dangerous die was never to be thrown for any of you! but, as probably it may, let me conjure you all, my dear girls, if ever any of you take this most important step in life, to proceed with the utmost care, and with deliberate circumspection. Fortune and family it is the sole province of your father to direct in; he certainly has always an undoubted right to a negative voice, though not to a compulsive one: as a child is very justifiable in the refusal of her hand, even to the absolute command of a father, where her heart cannot go with it, so is she extremely culpable in giving it contrary to his approbation. . . . The chief point to be regarded in the choice of a companion for life, is a really virtuous principle, an unaffected goodness of heart; without this, you will be continually shocked by indecency, and pained by impiety. So numerous have been the unhappy victims to the ridiculous opinion, "A reformed libertine makes the best husband," that, did not experience daily evince the contrary, one would believe it impossible for a girl, who has a tolerable degree of common understanding, to be made the dupe of so erroneous a position, which has not the least shadow of reason for its foundation, and which a small share of observation will prove to be false in fact. A man who has been long conversant with the worst sort of women is very apt to contract a bad opinion of, and a contempt for, the sex in general: incapable of esteeming any, he is suspicious of all; jealous, without cause, angry without provocation, and his own disturbed imagination is a continual source of ill-humor. . . . What rational prospect of happiness can there be with such a companion? and that this is the general character of those who are called reformed rakes, observation will certify; but, admit there may be some exceptions, it is a hazard, upon which no considerate woman would venture the peace of her whole future life. The vanity of those girls, who believe themselves capable of working miracles of this kind, and who give up their persons to men of libertine principles, upon the wild expectation of reclaiming them, justly deserves the disappointment which it will generally meet with; for, believe me, a wife is, of all persons, the least likely to succeed in such an attempt. Be it your care to find that virtue in a lover which you must never hope to form in a husband. Good sense and good nature are almost equally requisite; if the former is wanting, it will be next to impossible for you to esteem the person of whose behaviour you may have cause to be ashamed—and mutual esteem is as necessary to happiness in the married state, as mutual affection:—without the latter, every day will bring with it some fresh cause of vexation, till repeated quarrels produce a coldness which will settle into an irreconcileable aversion; and you will become, not only each other's torment, but the object of contempt to your family and to your acquaintance.

This quality of good nature is, of all others, the most difficult to be ascertained, on account of the general mistake of blending it with good humour, as if they were of themselves the same; whereas, in fact, no two principles of action are more essentially different—and this may require some explanation. By good nature, I mean that true benevolence which partakes the felicity of mankind, which promotes the satisfaction of every individual within the reach of its ability, which relieves the distressed, comforts the afflicted; diffuses blessings, and communicates happiness, as far as its sphere of action can extend; and which, in the private scene of life, will shine conspicuous in the dutiful son, in the affectionate husband, the indulgent father, the faithful friend, and in the compassionate master both to man and beast: whilst good humour, is nothing more than a cheerful, pleasing deportment, arising either from a natural gaiety of mind, or from an affectation of popularity, joined to an affability of behaviour—the result of good breeding, and a ready compliance with the taste of every company: this kind of mere good humour is, by far, the most striking quality; 'tis frequently mistaken for, and complimented with, the superior name of real good nature: a man, by this specious appearance, has often acquired that appellation, who, in all the actions of his private life, has been a morose, cruel, revengeful, sullen, haughty tyrant. . . . On the contrary, a man of a truly benevolent disposition, and formed to promote the happiness of all around him, may sometimes, perhaps from an ill habit of body, an accidental vexation, or from a commendable openness of heart, above the meanness of disguise, be guilty of little sallies of peevishness, or of ill-humour, which, carrying the appearance of ill-nature, may be unjustly thought to proceed from it, by persons who are unacquainted with his true character, and who take ill-humour and ill-nature to be synonymous terms; though in reality they bear not the least analogy to each other. In order to the forming a right judgment, it is absolutely necessary to observe this distinction, which will effectually secure you from the dangerous error of taking the shadow for the substance—an irretrievable mistake, pregnant with innumerable consequent evils!

From what has been said, it plainly appears, that the criterion of this amiable virtue is not to be taken from the general opinion;—mere good humour being, to all intents and purposes, sufficient, in this particular, to establish the public voice in favour of a man utterly devoid of every humane and benevolent affection of heart. It is only from the less conspicuous scenes of life, the more retired sphere of action, from the artless tenor of domestic conduct, that the real character can, with any certainty, be drawn—these, undisguised, proclaim the man; but, as they shun the glare of light, nor court the noise of popular applause, they pass unnoted, and are seldom known till after an intimate acquaintance: the best method, therefore, to avoid the deception in this case is, to lay no stress on outward appearances, which are too often fallacious, but to take the rule of judging from the simple, unpolished sentiments of those whose independent connexions give them an undeniable certainty—who not only see, but hourly feel, the good or bad effects of that disposition to which they are subjected. By this I mean, that if a man is equally respected, esteemed, and beloved by his tenants, by his dependants and domestics—from the substantial farmer to the laborious peasant—from the proud steward to the submissive wretch, who, thankful for employment, humbly obeys the menial tribe;—you may justly conclude, he has that true good nature, that real benevolence, which delights in communicating felicity, and enjoys the satisfaction it diffuses: but if, by these, he is despised and hated, served merely from a principle of fear devoid of affection—which is very easily discoverable, whatever may be his public character—however favourable the general opinion, be assured, that his disposition is such as can never be productive of domestic happiness. I have been the more particular on this head, as it is one of the most essential qualifications to be regarded, and of all others the most liable to be mistaken.

Never be prevailed with, my dear, to give your hand to a person defective in these material points: secure of virtue, of good nature, and understanding, in a husband, you may be secure of happiness: without the two former it is unattainable; without the latter in a tolerable degree, it must be very imperfect. (220–224)

Source: Hester Chapone, Dr. John Gregory, and Lady Pennington, *Chapone's Improvement of the Mind; Gregory's Legacy; Lady Pennington's Advice* (London: Scott and Webster, n.d.).

THOMAS GISBORNE

Thomas Gisborne, a contemporary of Austen, was a clergyman who is best remembered for two texts, *Enquiry into the Duties of Men in the Higher and Middle Classes of Society*, published in 1794, and *An Enquiry into the Duties of the Female Sex*, published in 1797. This latter text, like the conduct books by Dr. Gregory and Lady Pennington, addresses the subject of women's duties and responsibilities in marriage, but unlike their works, it stresses Biblical injunctions in its rationale for the restraints placed on women by marriage. Numerous conduct books of the age, like the one Mr. Collins reads to the Bennet girls, stressed Biblical injunctions over other considerations in their reasoning. Gisborne's was one of the most popular of that type.

Gisborne advocates the principle, based on the writings of St. Paul, of a wife's obedience to her husband. He does, however, allow one exception to that rule: "Were a husband presumptuously to require his wife to infringe the property or other rights of a third person, or to transgress any of the divine laws, she would be bound to obey God rather than man." Thus, the only situations in which Gisborne allows wives the right to disobey their husbands are those in which God's law or English property law (assumed to be God-given) clearly supercedes the desires of man.

Gisborne's *Enquiry* attaches a woman's destiny very tightly to her religious obligations and the spiritual attitude of the man she marries. Like Defoe at the beginning of the eighteenth century, Gisborne believes that a successful marriage can be founded only on strong spiritual compatibility and adherence to the laws of God.

FROM THOMAS GISBORNE, *AN ENQUIRY INTO THE DUTIES OF THE FEMALE SEX*
(London, 1797)

Whether marriage establishes between the husband and the wife a perfect equality of rights, or conveys to the former a certain degree of superiority over the latter, is a point not left among Christians to be decided by speculative arguments. The intimation of the divine will, communicated to the first woman immediately after the fall, is corroborated by various injunctions delivered in the New Testament. "Let the wife see that she reverence her husband.—Wives, submit yourselves unto your own husbands as unto the Lord; for the husband is the head of the wife, even as Christ is the head of the Church;—therefore, as the church is subject unto Christ, so let the wives be to their own husbands in every thing." The command in the second of these passages is so explicit, and illustrated by a comparison so impressive, that it is needless to recite other texts of a similar import. The obedience, however, which is here enjoined by the Apostle, is not unlimited obedience. Were a husband presumptuously to require his wife to infringe the property or other rights of a third person, or to transgress any of the divine laws, she would be bound to obey God rather than man. And it is very possible that he might be in other respects so unreasonable and injurious in this injunction, that she might with justice conceive herself exempted, as to those particular instances, from the obligation of implicit submission to his authority. St. Paul directs children to obey their parents, and servants their masters "in *all* things." Yet it is manifest that his direction was not intended to reach to things sinful, nor to other extreme cases which might be devised. It is reasonable, therefore, and it is also conformable to the general mode of conveying moral directions which is adopted in the Scriptures, to understand his strong declaration concerning the authority of a husband, as limited by restrictions and exceptions, corresponding to those with which his equally strong declarations concerning the authority of parents and of masters are manifestly to be understood. But though in cases such as have been supposed the duty of female obedience is suspended, it is suspended in these only. She who is commanded to "be subject to her head, the husband, as the church is subject to Christ, its head," cannot doubt that obedience, when it can innocently be rendered, is a branch of her connubial duty.

A branch of duty in its nature so important and extensive, ought to be considered antecedently to marriage with religious scrupulousness. And while the obligation is acknowledged, let not the ends for which it is imposed be misconceived. Let not pride or ignorance be for a moment permitted to suggest that the Father of the universe, in allotting obedience to the wife, has displayed a partial regard to the welfare and comfort of the husband. Eternal wisdom, incapable of error and of caprice, has in this dispensation consulted her happiness no less than that of her associate. If it were desirable to prevent or to lessen the bickerings, the conflicts, the pertinacious contrariety of plans and projects, which, in a state imperfect as human nature is, would perpetually arise and involve families in unceasing confusion, were each party free from any obligation to acquiesce in the decision of the other; by what method, were we to consult the dictates of unbiassed judgment, should we deem the object most likely to be attained? Undoubtedly by the method which Providence has adopted; by assigning to one of the partners in marriage a fixed preeminence over the other. If this point be once conceded, there cannot be room for much hesitation as to the only remaining question: to which of the two parties would it be wisest and best that the pre-eminence should be assigned? As the burden of the most laborious offices in life, of those offices which require the greatest exertions, the deepest reflection, and the most comprehensive judgments, is devolved upon man; and as man, that he may be qualified for the discharge of these offices, has been furnished by his creator with powers of investigation and of foresight in a somewhat larger measure than the other sex, who have been recompensed by an ample share of mental endowments of a different kind; it seems an appointment both reasonable in its nature and most conducive to the happiness, not only of the man himself, but of his wife, of his children, and of all his connections, that he should be the person to whom the superiority should be committed. But Heaven has not left the wife destitute or neglected. Security is provided for her in various ways against an arbitrary and tyrannical exercise of power on the part of the husband. Some limitations to which his authority is subjected have already been noticed. These he well knows. He knows too, that if he is entrusted with power, he acts under a proportionate responsibility, that he acts under the all-seeing eye of his future Judge. And if the Scriptures are on the one hand express in enjoining obedience to the wife, they are no less explicit on the other in reminding the husband of the mildness, the conciliating forbearance, the lively and never-failing tenderness of affection, which every branch of his behaviour towards his partner ought to display; and of the readiness with which he ought to make large sacrifices of personal inclination, ease, and interest, when essential to her permanent welfare. "Husbands, love your wives, and be not bitter against them." "Ye husbands, dwell with your wives according to knowledge; giving honour unto the wife, as unto the weaker vessel." "Husbands, love your wives, as Christ also loved the Church, and gave himself for it." If a woman marries a person without having sufficient reason to be satisfied, from actual knowledge of his character, that the commands of the Scriptures will decide his conduct, the fault surely is her own.

The foundation of the greater portion of the unhappiness which clouds matrimonial life, is to be sought in the unconcern so prevalent in the world, as to those radical principles on which character and the permanence of character depend,—the principles of religion. Popular language indicates the state of popular opinion. If an union about to take place, or recently contracted, between two young persons, is mentioned in conversation, the first question which we hear asked concerning it is, whether it be *a good match*. The very countenance and voice of the inquirer, and of the answerer, the terms of the answer returned, and the observations, whether expressive of satisfaction or of regret, which fall from the lips of the company present in the circle, all concur to shew what, in common estimation, is meant by being well married. If a young woman be described as thus married, the terms imply, that she is united to a man whose rank and fortune is such, when compared with her own or those of her parents, that in point of precedence, in point of command of finery and of money, she is, more or less, a gainer by the bargain. They imply, that she will now possess the enviable advantages of taking place of other ladies in the neighbourhood; of decking herself out with jewels and lace; of inhabiting splendid apartments; rolling in handsome carriages; gazing on numerous servants in gaudy liveries; and of going to London, and other fashionable scenes of resort, in a degree somewhat higher than that in which a calculating broker, after poring on her pedigree, summing up her property in hand, and computing, at the market price, what is contingent or in reversion, would have pronounced her entitled to them. But what do the terms imply as to the character of the man selected to be her husband? Probably nothing. His character is a matter which seldom enters into the consideration of the persons who use them, unless it, at length, appears in the shape of an afterthought, or is awkwardly hitched into their remarks for the sake of decorum. If the terms imply any thing, they mean no more than that he is not scandalously and notoriously addicted to vice. He may be proud, he may be ambitious, he may be malignant, he may be devoid of Christian principles, practice, and belief; or, to say the very least, it may be totally unknown whether he does not fall, in every particular, under this description; and yet, in the language and in the opinion of the generality of both sexes, the match is excellent. In like manner a small diminution in the supposed advantages already enumerated, though counterposed by the acquisition of a companion eminent for his virtues, is supposed to constitute a bad match; and is universally lamented in polite meetings with real or affected concern. The good or bad fortune of a young man in the choice of a wife is estimated according to the same rules.

From those who contract marriages, either chiefly, or in a considerable degree, through motives of interest or of ambition; it would be folly to expect previous solicitude respecting piety of heart. And it would be equal folly to expect that such marriages, however they may answer the purposes of interest or of ambition, should terminate otherwise than in wretchedness. Wealth may be secured, rank may be obtained; but if wealth and rank are to be main ingredients in the cup of matrimonial felicity, the sweetness of the wine will be exhausted at once, and nothing remain but bitter and corrosive dregs. When attachments are free from the contamination of such unworthy motives, it by no means always follows that much attention is paid to intrinsic excellence of moral character. Affection, quick-sighted in discerning, and diligent in scrutinizing, the minutest circumstances which contribute to shew whether it is met with reciprocal sincerity and ardor, is, in other respects, purblind and inconsiderate. It magnifies good qualities which exist; it seems to itself to perceive merits which, to other eyes, are invisible; it gives credit for what it wishes to discover; it enquires not, where it fears a disappointment. Yet, what security can a woman have for happiness in marriage, if the only foundation on which confidence can be safely reposed, be wanting? And ought she not, in common prudence, to consider it as wanting, until she is thoroughly convinced of its existence? He whose ruling principle is that of stedfast obedience to the laws of God, has a pledge to give, and it is a pledge worthy of being trusted, that he will discharge his duty to his fellow-creatures, according to the different relations in which he may be placed. Every other bond of confidence is brittle as a thread, and looks specious only to prove delusive. A woman who receives for her husband a person of whose moral character she knows no more than that it is outwardly decent, stakes her welfare upon a very hazardous experiment. She who marries a man not entitled even to that humble praise, in the hope of reclaiming him, stakes it on an experiment in which there is scarce a probability of her success. . . .

The truths which have been inculcated, are such as ought to be established in the mind while the affections are yet unengaged. When the heart has received an impression, reason acts feebly or treacherously. But let not the recent impression be permitted to sink deeper, ere the habitual principles and conduct of him who has made it shall have been ascertained. On these points in particular, points which a young woman cannot herself possess adequate means of investigating, let the advice and inquiries of virtuous relatives be solicited. Let not their opinions, though the purport of them should prove unacceptable, be undervalued; nor their remonstrances, if they should remonstrate, be construed as unkindness. Let it be remembered that, although parental authority can never be justified in constraining a daughter to marry against her will, there are many cases in which it may be justified in requiring her to pause. Let it be remembered, that if she should unite herself to a man who is unsettled as to the principles, or careless as to the practical duties of Christianity, she has to dread not only the risk of personal unhappiness from his conduct towards her, but the dangerous contagion of intimate example; she has to dread that his unsteadiness may render her unsteady, his carelessness may teach her to be careless. Does the prospect appear gloomy? Let her be wise, let her exert herself before it is too late. It is better to encounter present anxiety, than to avoid it at the expense of greater and durable evils. And even if affection has already acquired such force, as not to be repressed without very painful struggles; let her be consoled and animated by the consciousness that the sacrifice is to prevent, while prevention is yet in her power, years of danger and of misery; that it is an act not only of ultimate kindness to herself, but of duty to God; and that every act of humble and persevering duty may hope to receive, in a better world, a reward proportioned to the severity of the trial. (226–238, 240–242)

CRITICS OF THE STATUS QUO

WILLIAM GODWIN

While the majority of those who addressed the subject of matrimony in England at the end of the eighteenth century wrote in the same vein as the conduct books writers, not all agreed that marriage was a beneficial social institution. The opinions of William Godwin and Mary Wollstonecraft are very different from those of Thomas Gisborne, John Gregory, Lady Pennington, Hester Chapone, Hannah More, and other relatively conservative writers. The former depict not the ideal form of marriage, but what they consider to be its dominant real-world manifestations. In the following excerpt, William Godwin elaborates on what he perceives to be the evils of marriage as an institution.

As in most of *Enquiry Concerning Political Justice*, he advocates a complete overhaul of the existing social system, an aim of revolutionary proportions. Godwin had many followers in both England and France, and though the more conservative mainstream either disregarded his views or pronounced them perverse and immoral, many influential people of the early nineteenth century took seriously his ideas about marriage as part of the restructuring of society.

FROM WILLIAM GODWIN, *ENQUIRY CONCERNING
POLITICAL JUSTICE*
(London, 1793)

It is absurd to expect that the inclinations and wishes of two human beings should coincide, through any long period of time. To oblige them to act and to live together is to subject them to some inevitable portion of thwarting, bickering, and unhappiness. This cannot be otherwise, so long as man has failed to reach the standard [of] absolute perfection. The supposition that I must have a companion for life, is the result of a complication of vices. It is the dictate of cowardice, and not of fortitude. It flows from the desire of being loved and esteemed for something that is not deser[ved].

But the evil of marriage as it is practiced in European countries lies deeper than this. The habit is, for a thoughtless and romantic youth of each sex to come together, to see each other for a few times and under circumstances full of delusion, and then to vow to each other eternal attachment. What is the consequence of this? In almost every instance they find themselves deceived. They are reduced to make the best of an irretrievable mistake. They are presented with the strongest imaginable temptation to become the dupes of falsehood. They are led to conceive it their wisest policy to shut their eyes upon realities, happy if by any perversion of intellect they can persuade themselves that they were right in their first crude opinion of their companion. The institution of marriage is a system of fraud; and men who carefully mislead their judgments in the daily affair of their life, must always have a crippled judgment in every other concern. We ought to dismiss our mistake as soon as it is detected; but we are taught to cherish it. We ought to be incessant in our search after virtue and worth; but we are taught to check our inquiry, and shut our eyes upon the most attractive and admirable objects. Marriage is law, and the worst of all laws. Whatever our understandings may tell us of the person from whose connection we should derive the greatest improvement, of the worth of one woman and the demerits of another, we are obliged to consider what is law, and not what is justice.

Add to this that marriage is an affair of property, and the worst of all properties. So long as two human beings are forbidden by positive institution to follow the dictates of their own mind, prejudice is alive and vigorous. So long as I seek to engross one woman to myself, and to prohibit my neighbor from proving his superior desert and reaping the fruits of it, I am guilty of the most odious of all monopolies. Over this imaginary prize men watch with perpetual jealousy, and one man will find his desires and his capacity to circumvent as much excited as the other is excited to traverse his projects and frustrate his hopes. As long as this state of society continues, philanthropy will be crossed and checked in a thousand ways, and the still augmenting stream of abuse will continue to flow.

The abolition of marriage will be attended with no evils. We are apt to represent it to ourselves as the harbinger of brutal lust and depravity. But it really happens, in this as in other cases, that the positive laws which, in a state of equal property, would destroy the relish for luxury, would decrease our inordinate appetites of every kind, and lead us universally to prefer the pleasures of intellect to the pleasures of sense. . . .

It cannot be definitely affirmed whether it be known in such a state of society who is the father of each individual child. But it may be affirmed that such knowledge will be of no importance. It is aristocracy, self-love, and family pride that teach us to set a value upon it at present. I ought to prefer no human being to another because that being is my father, my wife, or my son, but because, for reasons which equally appeal to all understandings, that being is entitled to preference. (673–675)

Source: Raymond MacDonald Alden, ed. *Readings in English Prose of the Eighteenth Century*. Boston: Houghton Mifflin, 1911, 673–675.

MARY WOLLSTONECRAFT

One of Godwin's disciples, whom, ironically, he later married, was Mary Wollstonecraft, author of *A Vindication of the Rights of Woman*, who is generally considered one of the founders of the movement for women's rights in England and western Europe. In a novel left incomplete at her death, Wollstonecraft graphically illustrated the dangers of marriage for a woman.

Maria, or The Wrongs of Woman tells the story of Maria Venables, who has been severely mistreated by her husband. He has used her money to his advantage, has forced her to obtain additional money from her relatives, and has neglected her, cheated on her, and even convinced a friend to try to seduce her in return for money, actually attempting to sell her sexual services to him. When his machinations fail, he finally has her committed to a madhouse, intending to leave her there until she either cooperates in his schemes or dies.

By the end of the story, Maria has become involved with a man named Darnworth, also wrongly committed to the madhouse. Darnworth is arrested and put on trial for committing adultery with Maria, who then insists on having a statement of her own read into the trial transcript for the jury's consideration. In her statement she expresses her sense of the ethical legitimacy of her being legally independent of her husband. The law of the day, however, clearly states otherwise. The excerpt that follows includes her written statement and the response of the judge to it.

Wollstonecraft, like Godwin, views marriage as it was practiced in late eighteenth-century England as a trap and a fraud. Her character Maria presents her position quite clearly, but, as would the majority of people with any power in England at the time, the judge questions Maria's sanity and insists that "the sanctity of marriage" must be supported, even in the face of utter cruelty on the part of a spouse.

FROM MARY WOLLSTONECRAFT, *MARIA, OR THE WRONGS OF WOMAN* (1798)

"Married when scarcely able to distinguish the nature of the engagement, I yet submitted to the rigid laws which enslave women, and obeyed the man whom I could no longer love. Whether the duties of the state are reciprocal, I mean not to discuss; but I can prove repeated infidelities which I overlooked or pardoned. Witnesses are not wanting to establish these facts. I at present maintain the child of a maid servant, sworn to him, and born after our marriage. I am ready to allow, that education and circumstances lead me to think and act with less delicacy, than the preservation of order in society demands from women; but surely I may without assumption declare, that, though I could excuse the birth, I could not the desertion of this unfortunate babe:—and, while I despised the man, it was not easy to venerate the husband. . . . I exclaim against the laws which throw the whole weight of the yoke on the weaker shoulders, and force women, when they claim protectorship as mothers, to sign a contract, which renders them dependent on the caprice of the tyrant, whom choice or necessity has appointed to reign over them. Various are the cases, in which a woman ought to separate herself from her husband; and mine, I may be allowed emphatically to insist, comes under the description of the most aggravated.

"I will not enlarge on those provocations which only the individual can estimate; but will bring forward such charges only, the truth of which is an insult upon humanity. In order to promote certain destructive speculations, Mr. Venables [i.e., her husband] prevailed on me to borrow certain sums of a wealthy relation; and, when I refused further compliance, he thought of bartering my person; and not only allowed opportunities to, but urged, a friend from whom he borrowed money, to seduce me. On the discovery of this act of atrocity, I determined to leave him, and in the most decided manner, for ever. I consider all obligations as made void by his conduct; and hold, that schisms which proceed from want of principles, can never be healed.

"He received a fortune with me to the amount of five thousand pounds. On the death of my uncle, convinced that I could provide for my child, I destroyed the settlement of that fortune. I required none of my property to be returned to me, nor shall enumerate the sums extorted from me during six years that we lived together.

"After leaving, what the law considers as my home, I was hunted like a criminal from place to place, though I contracted no debts, and demanded no maintenance—yet, as the laws sanction such proceeding, and make women the property of their husbands, I forbear to animadvert. After the birth of my daughter, and the death of my uncle, who left a very considerable property to myself and child, I was exposed to new persecution; and, because I had, before arriving at what is termed years of discretion, pledged my faith, I was treated by the world, as bound for ever to a man whose vices were notorious. Yet what are the vices generally known, to the various miseries that a woman may be subject to, which, though deeply felt, eating into the soul, elude description, and may be glossed over! A false morality is even established, which makes all the virtue of women consist in chastity, submission, and the forgiveness of injuries.

"I pardon my oppressor—bitterly as I lament the loss of my child, torn from me in the most violent manner. But nature revolts, and my soul sickens at the bare supposition, that it could ever be a duty to pretend affection, when separation is necessary to prevent my feeling hourly aversion.

"To force me to give my fortune, I was imprisoned—yes; in a private mad-house.—There in the heart of misery, I met the man charged with seducing me. We become attached—I deemed, and ever shall deem, myself free. The death of my babe dissolved the only tie which subsisted between me and my, what is termed, lawful husband. . . .

"I claim then a divorce, and the liberty of enjoying, free from molestation, the fortune left to me by a relation, who was well aware of the character of the man with whom I had to contend.—I appeal to the justice and humanity of the jury—a body of men, whose private judgment must be allowed to modify law, that must be unjust, because definite rules can never apply to indefinite circumstances—and I deprecate punishment upon the man of my choice, freeing him, as I solemnly do, from the charge of seduction.

"I did not put myself into a situation to justify a charge of adultery, till I had, from conviction, shaken off the fetters which bound me to Mr. Venables.—While I lived with him, I defy the voice of calumny to sully what is termed the fair fame of woman.—Neglected by my husband, I never encouraged a lover; and preserved with scrupulous care, what is termed my honour, at the expence of my peace, till he, who should have been its guardian, laid traps to ensnare me. From that moment I believed myself, in the sight of heaven, free—and no power on earth shall force me to renounce my resolution."

The judge, in summing up the evidence, alluded to "the fallacy of letting women plead their feelings, as an excuse for the violation of the marriage-vow." For his part, he had always determined to oppose all innovation, and the new-fangled notions which incroached on the good old rules of conduct. We did not want French principles in public or private life—and, if women were allowed to plead their feelings, as an excuse or palliation of infidelity, it was opening a flood-gate for immorality. What virtuous woman thought of her feelings!—It was her duty to love and obey the man chosen by her parents and relations, who were qualified by their experience to judge better for her, than she could for herself. As to the charges brought against the husband, they were vague, supported by no witnesses, excepting that of imprisonment in a private madhouse. The proofs of an insanity in the family, might render that however a prudent measure; and indeed the conduct of the day did not appear that of a person of sane mind. Still such a mode of proceeding could not be justified, and might perhaps entitle the lady [in another court] to a sentence of separation from bed and board, during the joint lives of the parties; but he hoped that no Englishman would legalize adultery. . . . Too many restrictions could not be thrown in the way of divorces, if we wished to maintain the sanctity of marriage; and, though they might bear a little hard on a few, very few individuals, it was evidently for the good of the whole. (145–157)

Source: [Mary Wollstonecraft], *Posthumous Works of the Author of "A Vindication of the Rights of Woman,"* 4 vols. (London: J. Johnson, 1798).

Jane Austen's *Pride and Prejudice* was written within the context of all of these varying ideas about marriage and the duties of both men and women in regard to it. Clearly, her view of an appropriate husband for a gentlewoman is very close to that of Lady Pennington, as Fitzwilliam Darcy corresponds closely to Pennington's description of a model husband, and Elizabeth's prejudices regarding him correspond to those Lady Pennington cautions her own daughters to avoid. A clear interpretation of Austen's work, however, requires a knowledge of the different sides of the debate about the propriety of marriage as an institution and the expectations of society about the duties of husbands and wives, as well as an understanding of the legal status of men and women in marriage. Without such knowledge, the late twentieth-century reader of Austen cannot understand thoroughly the implications of all of the marital issues and marital relationships raised in *Pride and Prejudice* within the historical context in which the novel was written.

TOPICS FOR WRITTEN OR ORAL EXPLORATION

1. Write an essay in which you analyze Samuel Johnson's view about marriage being "not commonly unhappy, otherwise than as life is unhappy." Do you agree with his view? Do you disagree? Is his view as applicable today as it was in his own time? Explain.

2. Compare the process of courting in Jane Austen's time with the process of dating today. Which process do you think has the better chance of producing a successful marriage? Why?

3. Divorce in Austen's time was available only to the very rich, and only for a very limited number of reasons. As a result, marriage almost always continued until the death of one of the parties. Today in the United States, over half of the marriages entered into end in divorce. Which system do you think is more beneficial to personal happiness (remember to take into account the entire family's happiness, not just that of the individuals who are married to each other)? Which system do you think is more beneficial to society? Which system would you prefer to live under? Support your positions thoroughly.

4. In early nineteenth-century England, appropriate romantic behaviors were highly structured by gender. For example, it was acceptable for a woman to refuse a marriage proposal, but improper to propose to a man. It was considered proper for her to feel admiration for a man before he loved her, but improper to love him until he had asked her to marry him. Methods of proper flirting were gender-specific. Private time between men and women of marriageable age was highly restricted. Propriety was to be observed in the forms of address used with one another and in the degree of physical closeness allowed. Imagine dating under such rules of propriety. What, if anything, would you gain by such rules? What, if anything, would you lose? Explain your conclusions thoroughly.

5. Write an essay in which you compare the male-female "double standard" of romantic interaction in Austen's time to the male-female double standard of today. To what extent have things changed? To what extent are they the same? What are the implications of today's dating situation? How does the greater freedom of behavior benefit us as individuals? As a society? How does it harm us as individuals? As a society?

6. Write a response to Godwin's condemnation of marriage in *Enquiry Concerning Political Justice*. Are his views more or less appropriate to marriage as it is practiced today in the United States than they were to marriage as it was practiced in eighteenth-century England? Explain.

7. Gisborne, Gregory, and Pennington all advise their daughters about how and how not to choose husbands in the late eighteenth century. Write a letter of your own to a daughter or niece (actual or potential) advising her about choosing a marriage partner in the twenty-first century. Consider carefully all the issues you think would be important for her to be aware of, and present your views on them as clearly and persuasively as possible.

8. Many of the conduct books of the eighteenth century addressed the issue of women choosing husbands, but few writers seriously addressed the issues that men should consider in choosing wives. Write a letter to a son or nephew (actual or potential) advising him about choosing a marriage partner in the twenty-first century. Consider carefully all the issues you think would be important for him to be aware of, and present your views on them as clearly and persuasively as possible.

9. Some states in the United States are presently considering ways of making divorces more difficult to get as a way to encourage couples to work through their problems instead of ending their marriages, especially marriages that have produced children. Write an essay in which you present your own well-argued position on the topic of how difficult or easy obtaining divorce should be in your state.

SUGGESTED READINGS

Alden, Raymond MacDonald, ed. *Readings in English Prose of the Eighteenth Century*. Boston: Houghton Mifflin, 1911.

Armstrong, Nancy. *Desire and Domestic Fiction: A Political History of the Novel*. New York: Oxford University Press, 1987.

Blackstone, William. *Commentaries of the Laws of England*. London: John Murray, 1857.

Booth, George. *Considerations upon the Institution of Marriage*. New York: Garland Press, 1985.

Butler, Marilyn. *Jane Austen and the War of Ideas*. Oxford: Clarendon, Press, 1975.

Chandler, Alice. " 'A Pair of Fine Eyes': Jane Austen's Treatment of Sex." In *Jane Austen*. Edited by Harold Bloom. New York: Chelsea, 1986. 27–42.

Chapone, Hester, Dr. John Gregory, and Lady Sarah Pennington. *Chapone's Improvement of the Mind; Gregory's Legacy; Lady Pennington's Advice*. London: Scott and Webster, n.d.

Davidoff, Leonore, and Catherine Hall. *Family Fortunes: Men and Women of the English Middle Class, 1780–1850*. Chicago: University of Chicago Press, 1987.

Defoe, Daniel. *Conjugal Lewdness; or, Matrimonial Whoredom*. London: T. Warner, 1727.

Douglas, F[rancis]. *Reflections on Celibacy and Marriage*. New York: Garland Press, 1984.

Gilbert, Sandra M., and Susan Gubar. *The Madwoman in the Attic: The Woman Writer and the Nineteenth-Century Literary Imagination*. New Haven: Yale University Press, 1979.

Gisborne, Thomas. *An Enquiry into the Duties of the Female Sex*. London: T. Cadell, 1797.

Godwin, William. *Enquiry Concerning Political Justice*. London, 1793. Reprinted in *Readings in English Prose of the Eighteenth Century*. Edited by Raymond Macdonald Alden. Boston: Houghton Mifflin, 1911.

Hammerton, A. James. *Cruelty and Companionship: Conflict in Nineteenth-Century Married Life*. London: Routledge, 1992.

Hartcup, Adeline. *Love and Marriage in the Great Country Houses*. London: Sidgwick and Jackson, 1984.

Johnson, Claudia L. *Jane Austen: Women, Politics and the Novel*. Chicago: University of Chicago Press, 1988.

MacFarlane, Alan. *Marriage and Love in England: Modes of Reproduction, 1300–1840*. Oxford: Basil Blackwell, 1986.

Mews, Hazel. *Frail Vessels: Woman's Role in Women's Novels from Fanny Burney to George Eliot*. London: Athlone, 1969.

Monaghan, David. *Jane Austen in a Social Context*. Totowa, NJ: Barnes and Noble, 1981.

More, Hannah. *Essays on Various Subjects, Principally Designed for Young Ladies*. London: T. Cadell, 1791.

Newman, Karen. "Can This Marriage Be Saved?: Jane Austen Makes Sense of an Ending." *ELH* 50 (1983): 693–710.

Perkin, Joan. *Women and Marriage in Nineteenth-Century England*. London: Routledge, 1989.

Poovey, Mary. *The Proper Lady and the Woman Writer: Ideology as Style in the Works of Mary Wollstonecraft, Mary Shelley, and Jane Austen*. Chicago: University of Chicago Press, 1984.

Price, Martin. "Austen: Manners and Morals." In *Jane Austen*. Edited by Harold Bloom. New York: Chelsea, 1986. 163–78.

Staves, Susan. "Where Is History but in Texts?: Reading the History of Marriage." In *The Golden and the Brazen World. Papers in Literature and History, 1650–1800*. Edited by John M. Wallace. Berkeley: University of California Press, 1985. 125–44.

Stone, Lawrence. *Broken Lives: Separation and Divorce in England, 1660–1857*. Oxford: Oxford University Press, 1993.

———. *The Family, Sex, and Marriage in England, 1500–1800*. Oxford: Clarendon Press, 1984.

Sulloway, Alison G. *Jane Austen and the Province of Womanhood*. Philadelphia: University of Pennsylvania Press, 1988.

Swift, Jonathan. *The Works of Jonathan Swift Containing Additional Letters, Tracts, and Poems Not Hitherto Published with Notes and a Life of the Author by Sir Walter Scott*. Edited by Sir Walter Scott. 19 vols. 2nd ed. London: Bickers, 1883.

Trumbach, Randolph. *The Rise of the Egalitarian Family: Aristocratic Kinship and Domestic Relations in Eighteenth-Century England*. New York: Academic Press, 1978.

Weinsheimer, Joel. "Chance and the Hierarchy of Marriages in *Pride and Prejudice*." In *Jane Austen*. Edited by Harold Bloom. New York: Chelsea, 1986. 13–25

[Wollstonecraft, Mary.] *Posthumous Works of the Author of "A Vindication of the Rights of Woman."* 4 vols. London: J. Johnson, 1798.

4

Unmarried Women: Conduct and Law

Pride and Prejudice focuses on the importance of marriage to the lives of women of the gentry in late eighteenth- and early nineteenth-century England. When we focus exclusively on the issue of marriage in the novel, however, the fact that many women of Austen's time (including Austen herself) never married is often overlooked. In order to fully understand the significance of marriage for women like the Bennet sisters, a clear understanding of the alternatives is necessary. Life for women without husbands (permanently single women and widows) was very different from life for those with living mates.

"OLD MAIDS"

In the novel *Emma*, Austen creates a heroine who does not aspire to marriage. Like Charlotte Lucas, Emma Woodhouse seems to believe that happiness in marriage is a matter of chance, but unlike Charlotte, she does not need to marry to be secure financially. She does not choose to socialize beyond her own small town; therefore, the need to be chaperoned in society does not limit her movements. She is content with her life as the future heiress of one of the highest-ranking families in her neighborhood. Emma recognizes that she has no practical reason to marry, that, in fact, considering the law of the land, her independence would be seriously impinged upon if she were to wed. When her friend, Harriet Smith, wonders why she is not yet engaged, as would be expected of someone of her age and position, Emma responds:

> " 'I am not only, not going to be married, at present, but have very little intention of ever marrying at all. . . . I must see somebody very superior to any one I have seen yet, to be tempted . . . and I do *not* wish to see any such person. I would rather not be tempted. I cannot really change for the better. If I were to marry, I must expect to repent it.' " (76–77)

Emma recognizes that her position is both privileged and unusual. As her father's heir, with no brothers to take precedence over her, she will inherit his estate free and clear. Her sister has already given birth to a son who can be Emma's heir, so that, with no particular desire to have children of her own, she does not feel obligated to marry.

Despite Harriet's recognition that Emma's position is privileged, however, she continues to protest against Emma's determination not to marry, insisting that to be " 'an old maid' " is " 'so dreadful' " a fate that Emma cannot seriously consider it (77). But Emma is able to distinguish between her situation and that of other women: " 'I shall not be a poor old maid; and it is poverty only which makes celibacy contemptible to a generous public. . . . [A] single woman, of good fortune, is always respectable, and may be as sensible and pleasant as anybody else' " (77).

Emma's attitude is unusual in part because her situation is un-usual. Her fortune will prevent her from becoming a burden on her family or her community and enable her to lead an active life of useful employment as a spinster while enjoying family and com-munity connections. Emma recognizes that her financial and fa-milial position is especially fortunate. She knows that most women do not have her options.

In *Pride and Prejudice*, none of the young women at the center of the story are heiresses. In fact, all of the Bennet sisters, as well as Charlotte Lucas, need to marry to secure their financial futures. Austen's letters indicate her keen awareness of the problems of single women who become impoverished by the death of their parents, as the Bennet sisters would if their father died before they married. She writes her niece Fanny Knight about a Miss Milles whose mother has just died, leaving very little property behind: "I am sorry and surprised that you speak of her as having so little to leave, and must feel for Miss Milles . . . if a material loss of Income is to attend her other loss.—Single Women have a dreadful pro-pensity for being poor—which is one very strong argument in fa-vour of Matrimony" (*Letters*, 483).

In Austen's time, women of the gentry who never married were expected to be permanently celibate and to conduct their lives in a way that served others. Unless they had an independent fortune, they were expected to reduce their own needs to the minimum necessary for respectable survival. Most spinsters of Austen's time had little income of their own and few ways of earning money respectably. Most relied on fathers, brothers, or uncles to supply what necessities they could not purchase with their own meager funds. Spinsters without family who could (or would) provide for them often were forced to go into service as governesses, school teachers, or companions to the aged and ill, positions that, while minimally respectable, generally lowered their social position even further.

A number of eighteenth-century essayists and conduct book writ-ers addressed the issue of permanently unmarried women. Some, like Mary Wollstonecraft, saw a need for better education for women, to enable them to support themselves in a wider variety of respectable professions than those currently available to them. Wollstonecraft went further than most, even suggesting that the double standard of moral behavior for men and women be made less rigid, that women not be condemned forever by a single slip of virtue any more than men were. Most, however, like William Hayley and Jane West, focused on admonishing single women to live morally upright lives in service to others, to think less about themselves and their own needs and desires than about how they could ease the lives of those around them and avoid the dangers of becoming hard and selfish in their single condition.

HAYLEY'S REFLECTIONS ON OLD MAIDS

One of the most extensive eighteenth-century treatises on the subject of the single woman is William Hayley's *A Philosophical, Historical, and Moral Essay on Old Maids*. Hayley, who presents himself as "A Friend to the Sisterhood," takes it upon himself to write three volumes of advice to spinsters, counseling them about how to behave most virtuously in the position in which they have found themselves and admonishing them to avoid what he perceives to be the usual pitfalls of their situation.

In the first excerpt of the document below, Hayley describes what he perceives to be the usual circumstances of the middle- or upper-class spinster. His description is fairly accurate for women of his time.

The second excerpt argues that spinsters suffer even more from insult than from the poverty and social restrictions. Here Hayley presents himself as someone who understands how callous and inconsiderate those are who make jokes at the expense of the old maid. In fact, however, his own lack of understanding is apparent throughout the text, as was noted by more than one writer responding to his essay. In his attempt to "support" the "sisterhood," he manages to insult them as proficiently as anyone by comparing them with the maimed and deformed. To equate spinsterhood with deformity or disfigurement rendered it something unnatural and suggested that a woman's life had meaning only in terms of breeding and raising children. Many women of the period resented this view, especially writers like Mary Wollstonecraft and Catherine Macaulay, who advocated that women receive a better, more practical education and have a greater variety of professions open to them should they choose not to marry.

Hayley's three-volume essay continues to insult single women with admonishments to avoid falling into what he perceives to be "the particular Failings of Old Maids": too much curiosity (especially about things that are none of their business), too much credulity (especially about their own attractiveness to the men around them), too much affectation (especially in their dress and ornamentation), and too much envy and ill nature. He also acknowledges a few good qualities associated with such women: ingenuity in their accomplishments (developed over years of having the leisure time to practice their artistic interests), patience (learned through years of disappointment over not being asked to marry), and a spirit of charity (among those old maids who have not allowed envy and ill nature to embitter their souls).

That Hayley believed himself to be friend to the sisterhood of old maids may seem odd to those reading his words more than two centuries after they were first published. In fact, however, Hayley's views about never-married women were quite common, among women as well as men. Thus, Austen's Harriet Smith can claim that life as an old maid is "so dreadful" a fate that Emma cannot possibly consider it, and Charlotte Lucas can easily decide to draw the obsequious Mr. Collins into a marriage proposal that she accepts gratefully. The dangers that marriage presented to a woman by means of the law of coverture seemed small indeed compared with those posed by spinsterhood, a state many considered to be unnatural, and nearly everyone considered one of the least fulfilling and satisfying kinds of life a human being could endure.

FROM WILLIAM HAYLEY, *A PHILOSOPHICAL, HISTORICAL, AND
MORAL ESSAY ON OLD MAIDS*
(London, 1785)

Let us take a survey of the circumstances which usually attend the Old Maid, at the time of her first acquiring that title. If she has received a polite education—and to such I address myself—it is probable, that after having passed the sprightly years of youth in the comfortable mansion of an opulent father, she is reduced to the shelter of some contracted lodging in a country town, attended by a single female servant, and with difficulty living on the interest of two or three thousand pounds, reluctantly, and perhaps irregularly, paid to her by an avaricious or extravagant brother, who considers such payment as a heavy incumbrance on his paternal estate. Such is the condition in which the unmarried daughters of English gentlemen are too frequently found. To support such a change of situation, with that chearfulness and content which several of these fair sufferers possess, requires a noble firmness, or rather dignity of mind; a quality which many illustrious men have failed to exhibit in a similar reverse, and which ought therefore to be doubly honourable in these its more delicate possessors; particularly when we add, that the mortifications of their narrow fortune must be considerably embittered by their disappointment in the great object of female hope. Without the minutest breach of delicacy, we may justly suppose, that it is the natural wish and expectation of every amiable girl, to settle happily in marriage; and that the failure of this expectation, from whatever causes it may arise, must be inevitably attended by many unpleasant, and many depressive sensations. (7–8)

. . .

The vexations of a contracted fortune, and the mortifying neglect with which the indigent are treated, however galling to a generous mind, are not evils, perhaps, so productive of pain, as that coarse and contemptuous raillery, with which the ancient maiden is perpetually insulted. Habit and discretion may teach her to be contented with a very scanty income, and a noble ingenuous pride is her natural remedy against the wounds of neglect; but she seems utterly destitute of all adequate defence against her most provoking and most active enemy, the incessant impertinence of indelicate ridicule. How often does the amiable Old Maid smart under the flippant jocularity of the unfeeling rustic merchant, or the boorish squire who never fail to comment on the variations of her countenance, repeatedly wonder why she does not get her a husband, and very kindly hint to her, with equal delicacy of sentiment and language, that if she does not take great care she will slip out of the world without answering the end of her creation! (16–17)

. . .

[T]o sneer at the ancient virgin, merely because she has a claim to that title is not only inconsistent with good-nature and good manners, but, in truth, a piece of cruelty as wanton and malicious as it is to laugh at the personal blemishes of any unfortunate being, who has been maimed by accident, or deformed from his birth. Just and obvious as this sentiment must appear, it occurs not to jokers of a certain class, who, having met with some ridiculous Old Maids, are tempted to make the whole sisterhood their standing jest. Perhaps the particular failings, which are commonly imputed to the Old Maid in general, may be found to arise from the peculiarity of her situation, and the injurious treatment she receives from the world. (18)

WEST'S REFLECTIONS ON SPINSTERS

In *Letters to a Young Lady*, published in 1806, Jane West writes of the lives of single women as being less bleak than many people of the time have thought. She asserts that spinsters could lead active, useful, and happy lives, especially if they have access to substantial financial resources. She recognizes, however, that numerous women who could live such lives do not do so.

West considers herself to be "not only the *advocate* but also the *monitor* of single ladies (92)." As such, she believes it to be her duty to correct single women who do not lead lives of complete propriety. Boasting of past romantic conquests is, West insists, a common indiscretion for spinsters, one that West believes only encourages the kind of ridicule that denigrates unmarried women most often.

In the event that a woman without a fortune of her own does not marry early, West's advice is to make herself as little dependent as possible for company, activity, and money. West, unlike many in her time, believed that a single woman should have a basic knowledge of finances and business, so that she could avoid excessive dependence. West recognized, however, that complete independence would be extremely difficult, if not impossible, for a single woman without a fortune of her own.

West does not advocate the life of a spinster over that of a wife, but she does present it as a reasonable and potentially happy alternative, especially at a time when marriage afforded women virtually no independence and often led them into considerable disillusionment.

FROM JANE WEST, *LETTERS TO A YOUNG LADY, IN WHICH THE DUTIES AND CHARACTER OF WOMEN ARE CONSIDERED*
(London, 1806, 2nd ed., 3 vols.)

It is a false and dangerous assertion, that single women must at best pass their lives in a dull mediocrity, removed indeed from lively griefs, but unacquainted with real enjoyment. Spinsters may be daughters, sisters, aunts, and friends, though they are not wives and mothers. Every one's experience can supply instances, wherein as much warmth of attachment and solicitude of attention have accompanied the fraternal, as ever hallowed the conjugal tie. How many helpless orphans have found maternal tenderness supplied by the attachment of an aunt! How many parents have perceived the joyless portion of extreme old age turned into the downy pillow of repose, by the assiduous watchfulness of an unconnected daughter! Friendship, too, may reign in the heart of the single woman with unrivalled influence; and the absolute power that she possesses over her time and property gives an extensive range to her patriotic and charitable exertions. Ladies who are thus circumstanced are the properest patronesses of public undertakings; they are the natural *protectors* of the friendless, and the proprietors of those funds to which genius and indigence have a *right* to apply. Destitute of nearer ties, and unfettered by primary obligations, the whole world of benevolence affords a sphere for their actions, and the whole circle of science offers to adorn their minds. It seems, indeed, difficult to pourtray a more enviable being, than a single woman possessed of affluence, who has passed through the tempest of youthful passions with untainted character, unvitiated temper, and unfettered heart. Let us allow her an active mind, sound judgment, good principles, and bodily activity; and we must rank her with those orders of superior beings who, though they "neither marry nor are given in marriage," are ever employed in executing the will and studying the works of God. (Vol. 3, 89–91)

· · ·

I especially wish to correct their propensity to relate their early conquests. As the poor lovers whom they killed by their cruelty at eighteen, must be long ere this "dead and rotten;" informing us that such a one expired under a frown, and that another fell into a moral disease on their returning him an unopened letter, is but tantamount, in the scale of interesting conversation, to the list of apoplexies and consumptions in an old bill of mortality. If these *fair murderers* are agreeable and worthy, we can readily conceive that their singleness proceeded more from choice than compulsion; if they are destitute of these recommendations, we shall not credit the narrative of their conquests, though the sheeted ghosts of sighing swains returned from the myrtle shades, and showed us their hearts transfixed with Cupid's arrows. (Vol. 3, 92–93)

· · ·

[W]omen, therefore, ought to accustom themselves to those pursuits and occupations which will render them less dependent on the other sex, or enliven those lonely hours of retirement which frequently fall to the lot of poorly portioned celibacy. It is not only necessary that [spinsters] should be economical, but that they should have a general knowledge of business and money transactions, at least sufficient to escape *imposition*. To this should be added, activity of mind, that they may avoid the ennui inseparable from idleness, and the diseases incident to a sedentary life. Improving study of all kinds is here a most valuable acquisition; and elegant accomplishments cannot be pursued with too much avidity, provided they do not injure the health. Great care should be taken to rebut the sarcasms of witlings and coquets; I do not say by a life of decorum—for I suppose myself addressing women of virtue—but by a style of *manners* and *dress* suitable to their years. They should scorn all ridiculous affectation of youth, all "hoisting the flag of distress," as a witty author provokingly terms the pink riband when it waves over the wrinkled brow of faded beauty. The observation extends to manners and amusements, as well as dress; and they should also be solicitous to bid farewell to the allowable levities of youth, with that easy good-humour which shows that the resignation has not been painful. Let them but endeavour to be as useful to others as their limited means allow, and pursue every source of virtuous employment which their bounded sphere permits; and I can predict, that many a wife will have reason to envy the respectability and happiness of the old maid, and to regret that the silly ridicule attached to that name precipitated her into a ruinous and miserable connexion, which strength of mind would have enabled her to reject with the becoming pride of self-dependence. (Vol. 3, 93–96)

WOLLSTONECRAFT ON UNMARRIED WOMEN

In *Thoughts on the Education of Daughters*, published in 1787, Mary Wollstonecraft wrote extensively on the situation of fashionably educated women left without a fortune, and thus in need of earning their own living. Wollstonecraft knew this situation well, having been in it herself. Her description of the situation is, as a result, both explicit and emotional, and her observations carry more weight with many current readers than those of less emotionally charged writers. In her day, however, many considered her views less than rational. Her atypical way of life (living with a man without benefit of marriage and having his child; supporting the radical views of philosopher William Godwin; advocating women's rights, etc.) caused most readers of the day to avoid her works or, at the very least, to consider them tainted by her lifestyle.

The dilemma she presents in the following excerpt, that of a single woman of fashionable education forced into making a living for herself, vividly depicts some of the dangers of single life for a woman of Austen's time. If a single woman of the gentry had no income from inheritance and no family members to take her in, she was dependent upon the kindness of strangers, as she worked for them in a position socially higher than a servant but lower than the family. As a result, she lived in a kind of limbo, having no equals within the household, dependent on the good wishes of her employer, and subject to dismissal from service at a moment's notice.

FROM MARY WOLLSTONECRAFT, *THOUGHTS ON THE
EDUCATION OF DAUGHTERS: WITH REFLECTIONS ON FEMALE
CONDUCT, IN THE MORE IMPORTANT DUTIES OF LIFE*
(London, 1787)

[M]any who have been well, or at least fashionably educated, are left without a fortune, and if they are not entirely devoid of delicacy, they must frequently remain single.

Few are the modes of earning a subsistence [for those women], and those very humiliating. Perhaps to be an humble companion to some rich old cousin, or what is still worse, to live with strangers, who are so intolerably tyrannical, that none of their own relations can bear to live with them, though they should even expect a fortune in reversion. It is impossible to enumerate the many hours of anguish such a person must spend. Above the servants, yet considered by them as a spy, and ever reminded of her inferiority when in conversation with the superiors. If she cannot condescend to mean flattery, she has not a chance of being a favorite; and should any of the visitors take notice of her, and she for a moment forget her subordinate state, she is sure to be reminded of it.

Painfully sensible of unkindness, she is alive to every thing, and many sarcasms reach her, which were perhaps directed another way. She is alone, shut out from equality and confidence, and the concealed anxiety impairs her constitution; for she must wear a cheerful face, or be dismissed. The being dependant on the caprice of a fellow-creature, though certainly very necessary in this state of discipline, is yet a very bitter corrective, which we would fain shrink from.

A teacher at a school is only a kind of upper servant, who has more work than the menial ones.

A governess to young ladies is equally disagreeable. It is ten to one if they meet with a reasonable mother; and if she is not so, she will be continually finding fault to prove she is not ignorant, and be displeased if her pupils do not improve, but angry if the proper methods are taken to make them do so. The children treat them with disrespect, and often with insolence. In the mean time life glides away, and the spirits with it; "and when youth and genial years are flown," they have nothing to subsist on; or, perhaps, on some extraordinary occasion, some small allowance may be made for them, which is thought a great charity.

The few trades which are left, are now gradually falling into the hands of the men, and certainly they are not very respectable.

It is hard for a person who has a relish for polished society, to herd with the vulgar, or to condescend to mix with her former equals when she is considered in a different light. What unwelcome heart-breaking knowledge is then poured in on her! I mean a view of the selfishness and depravity of the world; for every other acquirement is a source of pleasure, though they may occasion temporary inconveniences. How cutting is the contempt she meets with!—A young mind looks around for love and friendship; but love and friendship fly from poverty: expect them not if you are poor! The mind must then sink into meanness, and accommodate itself to its new state, or dare to be unhappy. Yet I think no reflecting person would give up the experience and improvement they have gained, to have avoided the misfortunes; on the contrary, they are thankfully ranked amongst the choicest blessings of life, when we are not under their immediate pressure.

How earnestly does a mind full of sensibility look for disinterested friendship, and long to meet with good unalloyed. When fortune smiles they hug the dear delusion; but dream not that it is one. The painted cloud disappears suddenly, the scene is changed, and what an aching void is left in the heart! a void which only religion can fill up—and how few seek this internal comfort!

A woman, who has beauty without sentiment, is in great danger of being seduced; and if she has any, cannot guard herself from painful mortifications. It is very disagreeable to keep up a continual reserve with men she has been formerly familiar with; yet if she places confidence, it is ten to one but she is deceived. Few men seriously think of marrying an inferior; and if they have honor enough not to take advantage of the artless tenderness of a woman who loves, and thinks not of the difference of rank, they do not undeceive her until she has anticipated happiness, which, contrasted with her dependant situation, appears delightful. The disappointment is severe; and the heart receives a wound which does not easily admit of a compleat cure, as the good that is missed is not valued according to its real worth: for fancy drew the picture, and grief delights to create food to feed on.

If what I have written should be read by parents, who are now going on in thoughtless extravagance, and anxious only that their daughters may be *genteelly educated*, let them consider to what sorrow they expose them; for I have not over-coloured the picture. (69–77)

In 1792 Wollstonecraft published her women's rights manifesto, *A Vindication of the Rights of Woman*, in which she writes more fully about what women should be allowed to do to prepare themselves for life. Such preparation would, she asserts, protect unmarried women from the kind of morally and physically dangerous situation detailed in *Thoughts on the Education of Daughters*. She asks her readers to consider how unmarried women are supposed to care for themselves when they are educated for marriage, not for life.

Wollstonecraft suggests that instead of focusing on developing skills by which to amuse men, women develop skills with which they can support themselves respectably and profitably, not as underpaid and unrespected companions, governesses, or teachers.

Wollstonecraft's *A Vindication of the Rights of Woman* is often seen as the initial document of the modern movement for women's rights. Wollstonecraft saw herself, however, not as an innovator but as one continuing the movement for the rights of the individual, which was well under way by the time she wrote and had been an essential part of both the American and French Revolutions of the eighteenth century. In writing about the need to educate women for independent lives, she was extending the century's focus from the rights of the individual man to that of the individual human being. Her words created quite a stir, as they sowed the seeds of the women's rights movement to come, but it was another hundred years before British society was to change sufficiently to begin to enact her ideas for most women of the gentry.

FROM MARY WOLLSTONECRAFT, *A VINDICATION OF THE RIGHTS OF WOMAN WITH STRICTURES ON POLITICAL AND MORAL SUBJECTS*
(Boston, 1792)

Women might certainly study the art of healing, and be physicians as well as nurses. And midwifery, decency seems to allot to them, though I am afraid the word midwife, in our dictionaries, will soon give place to *accoucheur* [a male physician who presides at childbirth]. . . .

They might, also, study politics, and settle their benevolence on the broadest basis, for the reading of history will scarcely be more useful than the perusal of romances, if read as mere biography; if the character of the times, the political improvements, arts, &c. be not observed. . . .

Business of various kinds, they might likewise pursue, if they were educated in a more orderly manner, which might save many from common and legal prostitution. Women would not then marry for a support, as men accept of places under government, and neglect the implied duties; nor would an attempt to earn their own subsistence, a most laudable one! sink them almost to the level of some of those poor abandoned creatures who live by prostitution. For are not milliners and mantuamakers reckoned the next class? The few employments open to women, so far from being liberal, are menial; and when a superiour education enables them to take charge of the education of children as governesses, they are not treated like the tutors of sons, though even clerical tutors are not always treated in a manner calculated to render them respectable in the eyes of their pupils, to say nothing of the private comfort of the individual. But as women educated like gentlewomen, are never designed for the humiliating situation which necessity sometimes forces them to fill; these situations are considered in the light of a degradation; and they know little of the human heart, who need to be told, that nothing so painfully sharpens sensibility as such a fall in life.

Some of these women might be restrained from marrying by a proper spirit of delicacy, and others may not have had it in their power to escape in this pitiful way from servitude; is not that government then very defective, and very unmindful of the happiness of one half of its members, that does not provide for honest, independent women, by encouraging them to fill respectable stations? . . .

It is a melancholy truth; yet such is the blessed effect of civilization! the most respectable women are the most oppressed; and, unless they have understandings far superiour to the common run of understandings, taking in both sexes, they must, from being treated like contemptible beings, become contemptible. How many women thus waste life away the prey of discontent, who might have practised as physicians, regulated a farm, managed a shop, and stood erect, supported by their own industry, instead of hanging their heads surcharged with the dew of sensibility, that consumes the beauty to which it at first gave lustre; nay, I doubt whether pity and love are so near akin as poets feign, for I have seldom seen much compassion excited by the helplessness of females, unless they were fair; then, perhaps, pity was the soft handmaid of love, or the harbinger of lust.

How much more respectable is the woman who earns her own bread by fulfilling any duty, than the most accomplished beauty!—beauty did I say?—so sensible am I of the beauty of moral loveliness, or the harmonious propriety that attunes the passions of a well-regulated mind, that I blush at making the comparison; yet I sigh to think how few women aim at attaining this respectability by withdrawing from the giddy whirl of pleasure, or the indolent calm that stupifies the good sort of women it sucks in.

Proud of their weakness, however, they must always be protected, guarded from care, and all the rough toils that dignify the mind.—If this be the fiat of fate, if they will make themselves insignificant and contemptible, sweetly to waste "life away," let them not expect to be valued when their beauty fades, for it is the fate of the fairest flowers to be admired and pulled to pieces by the careless hand that plucked them. . . . Would men but generously snap our chains, and be content with rational fellowship instead of slavish obedience, they would find us more observant daughters, more affectionate sisters, more faithful wives, more reasonable mothers—in a word, better citizens. We should then love them with true affection, because we should learn to respect ourselves. (258–262)

"FALLEN" WOMEN

The dangers of singleness for women of the gentry and aristocracy were not only financial. The culture insisted on the "respectability" of women, which meant that any woman who engaged in sexual activity or even the appearance of sexual activity without marriage was considered "fallen." Once a woman had lost her respectability, her opportunities in life were so far reduced that she could not ever expect to marry (unless her seducer could be coaxed into marrying her) or to hold a position as governess, teacher, or paid companion.

Lydia Bennet's eventual marriage to Wickham in *Pride and Prejudice* is necessary for a happy ending to the novel. If Wickham had not been coerced and bribed into agreeing to marry her after running away with her, her chances of marrying or being received in respectable society would be at an end. Her belief that they were eloping in order to marry would not save her from being classified as "fallen." In Austen's novel *Mansfield Park*, Maria Bertram Rushworth, after her marriage to a boring but wealthy man, runs off with a man not her husband. Her future, once she is deserted by her lover, is determined by the extent to which her family will agree to care for her. Her family takes her in, but they condemn her to a quiet life in the country, watched over by her irritating and intrusive Aunt Norris. Such a destiny is the best that a single woman who did not adhere to society's rules about chastity could expect in the early nineteenth century.

The following news story from the *British Chronicle, or Pugh's Hereford Journal*, January 31, 1771, represents a more dire but not unusual result of seduction:

Leeds, Jan. 22. One night last week, a young woman hanged herself in a barn at Wetherby. The cause of her committing this rash action is said to be this; she had unfortunately suffered a young fellow, who courted and had promised to marry her, to get her with child; but he afterwards villainously deserting her, and her parents inconsiderately turning her out of doors, she determined to release herself from present misery, by putting a period to her life.

Women of high rank in society were usually somewhat protected from the worst results of seduction. If both the woman and her seducer were unmarried, and if the family of the woman was willing to make a deal with the seducer that was to his advantage, a hasty marriage could be arranged, as it is with Lydia Bennet and Wickham. Women of high rank also tended to be more protected within their families and schools from opportunities for elopement, chaperones being required for most encounters between young women and potential suitors. But women of the middle and lower ranks of society often had to be extremely careful to preserve their respectability. Many men of the day saw nothing wrong with seducing a servant, the daughter of a tenant, or a young woman in town who had no family ties among the elite. In 1786 the *Gentleman's Magazine* noted the frequency with which this practice occurred:

> There is nothing more common than to hear youth of *modern honour* and *fashion* use this argument for seduction: "Why, such a plan, no doubt, would have been disgraceful and infamous to have attempted upon a woman of *rank* and *fashion*!—but to an ordinary girl, and below one's rank, Lord! where's the harm?" . . .
> "I consider those below me as born to be subservient to me; and I think there is no harm in seducing a girl that is not entitled to expect me for a husband. If she allows liberties in such expectations, she is a fool."

The essay implies a condemnation of such attitudes, but even the condemnation is slight. The author suggests that there is, in fact, a problem with such an attitude, but that the attitude is so widespread and so generally accepted that there is little hope of changing it. The best a young woman can do, implies the author, is to be aware of such attitudes and increase her vigilance against potential seducers.

WIDOWS

A widow, of course, has not always been single, but she does share the spinster's financial independence when she is left well provided for and the prospect of poverty and downward-spiralling social standing when she is not.

The role of the widow in Austen's fiction is an important one. Widows in eighteenth- and nineteenth-century England, like spinsters, had an independent identity under the law that wives did not: they could own property and make wills regarding whatever portion of their property had not previously been disposed of by their husband's will or by entailment; they could choose where to live and spend their money as they saw fit. As with spinsters, however, these freedoms were enjoyed only by those who had sufficient property and income to be self-supporting. In Austen's novels, many of the most powerful women are, in fact, wealthy widows. But despite their fortunes, they never achieve the same degree of power in society as men with similar fortunes.

Lady Catherine de Bourgh of *Pride and Prejudice* is the woman with the most political and financial power in all of Austen's fiction. She rules her domain with an iron fist:

Elizabeth soon perceived that though this great lady was not in the commission of the peace for the county, she was a most active magistrate in her own parish, the minutest concerns of which were carried to her by Mr. Collins; and whenever any of the cottagers were disposed to be quarrelsome, discontented or too poor, she sallied forth into the village to settle their differences, silence their complaints, and scold them into harmony and plenty. (150–151)

Lady Catherine acts as the head of her extended family, and in a very real sense she is. But there are limits to her power. For instance, although she is "a most active magistrate in her own parish," she has no legal authority as magistrate; being a woman, she is not commissioned as a peace officer. She may act the part, and her community may respond to her in that role, but she has no legitimate authority to resolve disputes, power that her late husband, as the most influential landed gentleman in the community, could easily have had if he wanted it.

That Lady Catherine disapproves of the tradition of primogeniture is illustrated by the way she quizzes Elizabeth about her family, only to pronounce strongly against the standard practice of entailment on collateral males (cousins and nephews): " 'I see no occasion for entailing estates from the female line. It was not thought necessary in Sir Lewis de Bourgh's family' " (146). And indeed, it was not. If the de Bourgh estate had been entailed or strictly settled according to tradition to the next male in the family line, Lady Catherine would have had little or no power after the death of her husband, and her daughter would not be heir to the estate. Instead, the estate would have been turned over to her husband's male heir, and she and her daughter would have had to depend for their livelihood upon the widow's jointure (an annuity from the husband's estate allowed to a widow after his death) and daughter's portion (whatever amount of personal property the daughter inherited from her father). If the combination of the jointure and the daughter's portion was insufficient for their maintenance, the new male head of the family might, if he chose, assist the women through his benevolence. If he did not choose to assist them, they would have to manage with a drastically reduced lifestyle. Lady Catherine's power is, therefore, the result of her husband's family having settled the estate against tradition, leaving the family's fortune in the hands of Lady Catherine and her daughter.

The situation in which Lady Catherine finds herself as a widow was not typical in early nineteenth-century England. Few widows were left in complete control of estates. Instead, estates tended to pass from one generation of males to the next, and women were rarely allowed much control over even such portions as were theirs by law. More typical was the situation of Mrs. Jennings of *Sense and Sensibility*, a widow who has been left a substantial income but who does not control her late husband's estate.

Mrs. Jennings, we are told, is a widow, with "an ample jointure" (30). This single statement provides the reader with considerable information. In most cases, the jointure was in effect for the life of the widow, securing her future, giving her financial independence. Mrs. Jennings is fortunate in widowhood. Whereas poor widows like Mrs. Dashwood of the same novel must depend upon the kindness of relatives to sustain them, Mrs. Jennings can pay her own way. She can rent a house in London when she chooses; she can hire coaches for traveling, invite young women to stay with her as her guests, and indulge in matchmaking without thought of her own needs, which are provided for by her jointure.

A jointure could allow a widow independence for her lifetime, but it did not enable her to provide for others after her death. At her death, the income reverted to her late husband's estate. At one point in *Sense and Sensibility*, John Dashwood hypothesizes that Mrs. Jennings cares deeply enough about Elinor to leave her a legacy. Elinor finds his suggestion offensive, noting that there is no reason to expect that Mrs. Jennings should prefer to leave money to Elinor rather than to her own daughters. But even if she should care to leave something to the Dashwood women, Elinor points out, she would not be able to, " 'for she has only her jointure, which will descend to her children' " upon her death (198). Jointures could, therefore, give a widow considerable independence and autonomy for the rest of her life, but her power over others usually remained quite limited. She was not able to provide for others after her own death unless she had control of property other than her jointure, a situation that comparatively few widows of Austen's time enjoyed.

Not all widows were so well provided for. When a man's estate was entailed and he had little or no personal property (money, investments, or valuable possessions) that was not tied to the estate's entail, his widow could be left with little or no money. This would be the result upon Mr. Bennet's death, since he and his wife had lived to the extent of their means during their lifetime together. Mrs. Bennet and her daughters have only a small reserve of money that is being held in trust for them in the event of Mr. Bennet's death.

Austen creates the characters of widows with very narrow means in several of her novels. In *Emma* Mrs. Bates, the former clergyman's widow, is left with very small means, so small, in fact, that she finds it necessary to rent rooms from a local tradesman for herself and her spinster daughter. Her means are so small that she cannot even provide a home for her orphaned granddaughter, Jane Fairfax, who prepares herself for life as a governess through the benevolence of a friend of her late father. The Bates women are so stretched for financial support, in fact, that some of the local gentry actually supply them with food from time to time—respectfully, of course, never alluding to the poverty in which the women find themselves. Without such assistance from their community, however, the women would find themselves falling lower and lower, both socially and financially, as their small inheritance dwindles away.

LEGAL RIGHTS OF WIDOWS

In his 1779 treatise on the history of women, William Alexander details the legal rights of widowhood, in particular the financial rights of a widow. As he points out, a widow was assumed to have a right to a reasonable dower, that is, to inherit an amount sufficient to support a lifestyle suitable to her standing as the widow of a man of her husband's rank. Thus, the law entitled women to a portion of their late husband's estate as a jointure, but that entitlement applied only to property that a man owned outright, not property in which he had only a life tenancy (as is true of the Bennet estate). It also applied only to property that he owned outright at the time of his death, unless a previous settlement of property had been made upon his wife, usually held in trust by a family member until such time as the husband died. As a result, though the excerpt below indicates the historical development of a widow's legal right to sufficient support from her late husband's estate, the situation of each estate had to be treated individually, and women often did not receive the amount of support that the phrasing of the law would seem to indicate they deserved.

The common law right to a dower and the legal right to a jointure settled upon the widow by the marriage settlement meant that many widows continued to be provided for by their late husbands' estates. A widow, however, like a spinster, could find herself affluent, in abject poverty, or at any point in between, depending on her late husband's financial situation and on the competence of those who negotiated the marriage settlement. In general, a widow had a better chance of maintaining a standard of living comparable to what she had with her husband than a spinster had of maintaining a standard of living comparable to what she had in her father's house prior to his death, but both categories of women had their financial futures determined, to a large extent,

by the men upon whom they depended (or had previously depended) for maintenance.

FROM WILLIAM ALEXANDER, *THE HISTORY OF WOMEN FROM
THE EARLIEST ANTIQUITY, TO THE PRESENT TIME*
(London, 1779, 2 vols.)

When a woman, on her entrance into matrimony, gives up her fortune
to the power and discretion of her husband; or, perhaps, when she has
no fortune, when, through a long and tedious course of years, she joins
her own management, labour, and industry to his; nothing can be more
reasonable, than that she should be provided for, in case of his dying
before her; and it would be a capital defect in the laws of civil society,
to leave this provision altogether in the power of individuals, by whom
it might frequently be disregarded or neglected, and the widows even of
such husbands as had died in affluence, left to experience all the hard-
ships of want and poverty; to prevent which, the law of this country has
wisely ordered, that every widow shall have a reasonable dower out of
the effects or estates of her deceased husband, even though there was
no marriage-settlement, or though, in such settlement, no dower was
stipulated to the wife. . . .

Before marriage-settlements came so much into fashion, the dower
which was settled by the law, or with which the husband endowed the
wife at the time of marriage, was the only security she had for a maintenance, in case she became a widow. . . .

As dower, either by the common law or by the special custom of the
place, was frequently considered by the contracting parties as too great
or too little, the present times have hardly left any thing to run in that
channel, the parties thinking it better to stipulate and agree between
themselves on a specific quantity of land or money, which is, previous to
the marriage, settled upon the wife by way of jointure, and which effectually takes away all her right to any dower. The jointure, thus legally
settled, is still more inviolable to the wife than her dower; it cannot be
touched by the creditors of the husband; and though a dower be forfeited
by the husband being guilty of high-treason, a jointure is not. Every jointure must be made to the wife, for the term of her own natural life; if
made for the life of another person, it is not legal, and she may refuse
it, and claim the dower which the common law will assign her. (330–
334)

TOPICS FOR WRITTEN OR ORAL EXPLORATION

1. Write and produce a reader's theatre in which you have the characters of Elizabeth Bennet, Jane Bennet, Lydia Bennet, Charlotte Lucas, Miss Bingham, and Miss King discuss how different their lives would have been had they never married.

2. Write an alternative ending for the Lydia/Wickham affair, one in which the two do not marry. Be sure to be faithful to the social expectations of early nineteenth-century British society.

3. Project yourself into a future time, after Darcy's death, when Elizabeth is his widow. How do you think Elizabeth would behave as the wealthy widow of Fitzwilliam Darcy? In what ways would she compare to Lady de Bourgh? In what ways would she differ? Be sure to be faithful to the characters as they are depicted in the novel.

4. Imagine yourself as a single young woman of marriageable age in early nineteenth-century England. How determined do you think you would be to find a husband? To what lengths would you go to get married? How would you react to the possibility of becoming an old maid?

5. Consider the stereotypes associated with spinsters in the late eighteenth and early nineteenth centuries (as expressed by Hayley, West, and others). Then compare those stereotypes to the stereotypes associated with women who never marry today. What do the images have in common? In what ways do they differ?

6. Create a list of characteristics that you associate with the terms "spinster" or "old maid." Then create a list of characteristics that you associate with the word "bachelor." Which characteristics do the lists share? Which characteristics are found on only one list? What does an examination of the lists tell you about the values society teaches about unmarried women and unmarried men? Write an essay explaining your conclusions.

7. In Austen's time, a woman's chastity was often considered to be her most prized possession. A "fallen" woman was usually considered to be unmarriageable and permanently disreputable. What are the benefits of a system that puts such a high value on female chastity? What are the disadvantages of such a system? Divide the class into two teams, one to argue in support of the early nineteenth-century value system regarding female chastity as important to a society's well-being, and one to argue that such a value system is detrimental to the society's well-being on the whole. After giving both groups time to gather their ideas, stage a debate on the issue.

8. In the early nineteenth century, men of the middle and upper classes

were often encouraged to "adventure" by traveling, dabbling in various love affairs, and participating in other worldly activities in order to gain experience. Women of those classes, on the other hand, were usually restricted in their travels, were encouraged to keep potential suitors at arm's length (while, of course, enticing them into proposals of marriage), and were to avoid any worldly activity that could threaten the appearance of innocence and respectability in their lives. Write a brief play in which childhood acquaintances of Austen's time, one male and one female, neither of whom ever married, meet in old age and discuss their lives with each other. Note the differences that are based on social expectation and experience as well as any differences associated with the personalities of the characters you create.

SUGGESTED READINGS

Alexander, William. *The History of Women from the Earliest Antiquity, to the Present Time*. 2 vols. London: W. Strahan and T. Cadell, 1779.

Austen, Jane. *Emma*. New York: Oxford University Press, 1990.

———. *Sense and Sensibility*. New York: Oxford University Press, 1990.

Copeland, Edward. "What's a Competence? Jane Austen, Her Sister Novelists, and the 5%'s." *Modern Language Studies* 9 (1979): 161–68.

Davidoff, Leonore, and Catherine Hall. *Family Fortunes: Men and Women of the English Middle Class, 1780–1850*. Chicago: University of Chicago Press, 1987.

Douglas, Francis. *Reflections on Celibacy and Marriage*. Reprint. New York: Garland Press, 1984.

The Female Aegis; or, the Duties of Women from Childhood to Old Age, and in Most Situations of Life, Exemplified. London, 1798.

Gisborne, Thomas. *An Enquiry into the Duties of the Female Sex*. London: T. Cadell, 1797.

Hayley, William. *A Philosophical, Historical, and Moral Essay on Old Maids*. London: T. Cadell, 1785.

Hays, Mary. *Appeal to the Men of Great Britain on Behalf of Women*. London, 1798.

The Laws Respecting Women: as They Regard Their Natural Rights, or Their Connections and Conduct. London, 1777.

Malcomson, A.P.W. *The Pursuit of the Heiress: Aristocratic Marriage in Ireland, 1750–1820*. Belfast: Ulster Historical Foundation, 1982.

A Master-Key to the Rich Ladies Treasury; or, The Widower and Batchelor's Directory: Containing an Exact Alphabetical List of the Duchess, Marchioness, Countess, Viscountess, Baroness Dowagers, Ladies. London, 1742.

Mews, Hazel. *Frail Vessels: Woman's Role in Women's Novels from Fanny Burney to George Eliot*. London: Athlone, 1969.

Price, Richard. *Observations on Reversionary Payments: On Schemes for Providing Annuities for Widows, and for Persons in Old Age; On the Method of Calculating the Values of Assurances on Lives; and On the National Debt*. London, 1771.

Stone, Lawrence. *Broken Lives: Separation and Divorce in England, 1660–1857*. New York: Oxford University Press, 1995.

West, [Jane]. *Letters to a Young Lady, in which the Duties and Character of Women Are Considered*. 3 vols. 2nd ed. London, 1806.

Wollstonecraft, Mary. *Thoughts on the Education of Daughters: With Reflections on Female Conduct, in the More Important Duties of Life*. London, 1787.

———. *A Vindication of the Rights of Woman with Strictures on Political and Moral Subjects*. Boston, 1792.

5

Women's Education and Moral Conduct

In late eighteenth- and early nineteenth-century England, education was handled very differently from how it is today. There was no such concept as universal education whereby every child is considered to have a right to a formal education, and the government is obliged to provide one if the parents cannot. The kind and amount of education a child received in Austen's time depended on several factors: the social level of the family, the value that family (especially the father) placed on education, the financial situation of the family, and the gender of the child.

In each level of British society, the formal education of daughters was considered of less importance than the formal education of sons. On the one hand, men of the aristocracy and upper gentry were often educated at highly regarded schools such as Eton and often attended university, sometimes in order to prepare themselves for a profession, sometimes to establish themselves among other young men of their social standing. Women, on the other hand, had no schools of recognized academic excellence available to them and were ineligible for university attendance because of their sex. A woman's education, therefore, even among the higher classes, remained less uniform and of less importance (theoretically, at least) to her future than a man's was.

Women of the gentry were often educated at home by their

mothers or by governesses. Male tutors were occasionally brought in to teach some subjects, but most women were taught exclusively by women. Their studies generally focused on ornamental accomplishments and housewifery rather than academics. Though an ability to read and to do basic sums (sufficient for keeping track of the housekeeping accounts) was considered appropriate for a young woman of the upper gentry and the aristocracy, a significant amount of her educational time was spent attaining such accomplishments as playing the piano, singing, embroidering, dancing, drawing, and painting. Women of the lower gentry and the working classes were taught the rudiments of housekeeping, including sewing and cooking (in order to supervise staff or to do the work themselves) as well as whatever ornamental accomplishments could be inexpensively learned and practiced to make them fit companions for men of small means, or to be used if they became servants themselves.

Because academic education was considered a luxury for most women (and was even considered a threat to women's health by many), many treatises of Austen's time on the education of women addressed issues that we would not today define as purely educational. Guidance about moral behavior, proper attitudes, proper dress, and prospective marriage partners was part of a young woman's "education." What books she read to help her develop into an attractive marital partner was of more importance to many people than what books she read to develop her intellect. Dancing, drawing, and musical performance were considered more useful than the development of critical thinking skills and common sense in the young woman; the expectation was that the former would more readily attract eligible young men. Learning to enhance one's beauty to lure as many potential suitors as possible was thought more important than learning skills that might enable a woman of the gentry or aristocracy to support herself financially in the future.

Many writers debated the issue of what constituted the most appropriate education for a young woman. Some focused on a woman's need to prepare herself for marriage, others on her need to learn how to be marriageable. The preparations for these states differed considerably. In marriage, a woman generally had to supervise (if not perform) all of the household activities, from cooking and cleaning to growing and purchasing food for the table and keeping tabs on the household accounts. A woman whose education focused on preparation for marriage as an ongoing life commitment was generally more able to be a good helpmate to her husband because of the practicality of what she had learned. If, however, her husband had any pretensions to gentility, the woman, no matter how proficient in running a household, would also be expected to be "accomplished." A woman who had not developed a variety of ornamental accomplishments might well never marry, no matter how well her education had prepared her for running a household.

By the same token, a woman whose education focused exclusively or nearly exclusively on accomplishments (on being marriageable) might find herself very popular among her genteel suitors, but utterly unprepared to deal with the day-to-day supervision of a household after marriage. If her husband was wealthy and wise enough to have a loyal housekeeper and steward, her purely ornamental education might not present a serious problem. Her beauty and accomplishments, however, might wear thin in time if she did not also possess common sense and practical household skills. Mrs. Bennet of *Pride and Prejudice* is a most vivid example of that possibility. She initially attracted her husband by her beauty and lightheartedness, but her inability to run a household efficiently, together with her lack of intellectual knowledge and common sense, eventually causes her husband to regret having married her, to ridicule her in front of her own children, and to avoid spending time in her presence whenever possible.

VIEWS ON WOMEN'S EDUCATION

Excerpts from five eighteenth- and nineteenth-century English texts follow. William Alexander, in his *History of Women*, discusses the negative effects of contemporary methods of education for women, but he does not suggest specific solutions to the problem. Hester Chapone, Lady Sarah Pennington, and Jane West all propose very specific strategies for educating women to prepare them for their place in the world. Chapone's focus is on preparing to run a household and to be a good helpmate to a husband. Lady Pennington's intent is similar, but her approach is more accepting of women's exploration of their intellect than is Chapone's. West focuses particularly on the need for young women to be thoroughly and carefully trained in Christian precepts and practices in order that they may navigate the dangerous waters of society successfully. Catherine Macaulay's treatise differs significantly from the others. She directly attacks the views of Jean-Jacques Rousseau and those whose educational philosophies, like Rousseau's, insist on separate and unequal education for males and females. Macaulay strongly advocates equal education for both sexes, suggesting that only equality of education can adequately prepare both men and women for their roles in creating a more productive and progressive future.

WILLIAM ALEXANDER

In his 1779 history of women, William Alexander writes of the complaints so many men of Austen's time made about the young women available to them as potential marriage partners: complaints about their lack of conversational skill on any issue of intellectual depth, about their overemphasis on dress and ornamentation, about their lack of understanding about the requirements of economy in the home and in the world of business. He agrees that the complaints are often valid. But instead of blaming the women themselves, he blames the education society encourages them to have. And this education, he asserts, is ultimately the fault of men, who find themselves attracted to women of ornamental accomplishments rather than to women of substance.

"[W]e have never in any period, nor in any country," Alexander writes, "sufficiently attended to the happiness and interests of those beings, whom in every period, and in every country, we have professed to love and to adore; and while the charms which they possess, have every where extorted from us the tribute of love, they have only in a few places extorted from us good usage" (1).

In his condemnation of the state of female education, Alexander specifically addresses the standard education received by fashionable young women in many of the girls' boarding schools of England and Europe, which would probably be referred to as "finishing schools" today. Girls whose families chose to send them away to school instead of educating them at home with a governess often received precisely the kind of education Alexander describes in his *History*—one that did little to prepare them for lives as wives and mothers.

Alexander writes of the situation as he perceived it in the late eighteenth century, but he does not propose any specific plan for female education that could replace and correct the faulty curriculum. He identifies specific problem areas, but leaves it to others to propose potential remedies for the situation.

FROM WILLIAM ALEXANDER, *THE HISTORY OF WOMEN FROM THE EARLIEST ANTIQUITY, TO THE PRESENT TIME*
(London, 1779, 2 vols.)

Almost every man is full of complaints about the sex, but hardly do we meet with any one who seriously endeavours to rectify the evils against which he exclaims so bitterly. He who considers women only as objects of his love, and of his pleasure; complains, that in his connections with them, he finds them inconstant, unfaithful, and ever open to flattery and seduction. The philosopher, who would wish to mingle the joys of friendship and of conversation with those of love, complains that they are destitute of every idea, but those that flow from gallantry and self-admiration; and consequently incapable of giving or receiving any of the more refined and intellectual pleasures. The man of business complains, that they are giddy and thoughtless, and want the plodding head, and the saving hand, so necessary towards thriving in the world. And almost every man complains, of their idleness, extravagance, disregard to every kind of admonition, and neglect of the duties of domestic and social life.

Without examining how far these general complaints are well or ill founded, we shall only observe, that in cases where they are well founded, when we trace them to their source, we find the blame ultimately falls on ourselves. Does not the man of love and gallantry commonly set the example of infidelity and inconstancy to the females with whom he is connected? And do not men in general, but too obviously, chalk out to the other sex, the way that leads to every levity and folly? What made the philosopher so susceptible of the rational and intellectual pleasure? doubtless, the education bestowed upon him; and the same education might have given his wife or his daughter, an equal, or even a superior relish for them; it is folly in him therefore to expect the fruit without the culture necessary to bring it to perfection. The plodding and steadiness of the man of business, he has acquired in his early years; and they are augmented by his being sole master of what he can amass, and having a power to spend or dispose of it as he thinks proper. But his wife was brought up in no such school, and has no such motives to industry; for should she even toil with the utmost assiduity, she cannot appropriate to herself what she acquires; nor lay out any part of it without leave of her husband. Nor is the idleness, extravagance, and neglect of domestic duties, which we so commonly charge upon the sex, so much the fault of nature as of education. Can we expect that the girl whom we train up in every fashionable levity and folly, whom we use our utmost efforts to flatter and to amuse, shall, the moment of her marriage, totally change her plan, and become the sober and economical housewife? as well might we sow weeds and expect to reap corn.

If this be, as we persuade ourselves it is, a candid and impartial state of the source of female folly and of female weakness; if the whole may be traced either to the total want of, or to an improper education; and if the power of neglecting this education altogether, or bestowing it improperly, be lodged in our hands, as having the sole management and direction of the sex; then it will follow, that we should act a much better and more becoming part, in trying to amend their faults by a more judicious instruction, than to leave them ignorant, and complain that they are so; or teach them folly, and rail at them for having learned what we taught them. But instead of doing this, in every age, and in every country, while the men have been partial to the persons of the fair, they have either left their minds altogether without culture, or biassed them by a culture of a spurious and improper nature; suspicious, perhaps, that a more rational one would have opened their eyes, shewn them their real condition, and prompted them to assert the rights of nature; rights of which the men have perpetually, more or less, deprived them. (1–3)

• • •

Should this imperfect attempt, to write the History of the Fair, survive the present, and be read in any future generation, when this frivolous mode of female education shall have given place to a better, that our readers may then have some idea of what it was towards the close of the eighteenth century, we shall just sketch the outlines of it as now prac- tised. . . . Among the first lessons, which a mother teaches her daughter, is that important article, according to the modern phrase, of holding up her head, and learning a proper carriage: this begins to be inculcated at the age of three or four at latest; and is strenuously insisted on for many years afterward. When the young lady has learned imperfectly to read her own language, and sometimes even sooner, she is sent to a boarding- school, where she is instructed in the most flimsy and useless parts of needlework; while of those, which she must need, if ever she enters into domestic life, she is left entirely ignorant. While she is here, some part of her time is also allotted to learning to read either her own language, or the languages of some of the neighbouring kingdoms; all of which are too frequently taught without a proper attention to Grammar or Orthog- raphy. Writing, and Arithmetic, likewise employ a part of her time; but these, particularly the last, are only considered as auxiliary accomplish- ments, which are not to be carried into life, and consequently deserve but little attention; the grand effort is generally made to teach the girl what the woman will relinquish; such as drawing, music, and dancing; these, as they are arts agreeable to youthful sprightliness, often engage the young lady so much, as to make her neglect, or forget every thing else. To these are added, the modes of dressing in fashion, the punctilios of behaving in company; and we are sorry to say, into some schools have been introduced masters to teach the fashionable games at cards; a dis- sipation, if not a vice, which already prevails too much among both sexes, and may perhaps still gain ground by this early initiation.

Such, in general, is the education of female boarding-schools; in some, indeed, there may be a few other things taught besides those we have mentioned; but whatever be taught, or however they be conducted, it is too true, that the girl, after having been there some years, comes home to her parents quite a modern fine lady; with her head full of scraps of French, names of great people, and quotations from romances and plays; and quite disgusted at the antiquated virtues of sober frugality, order or economy. We cannot cast our eyes on the picture we have now drawn, without a secret wish, that it were less just; nor shall we drop the curtain before it, without mentioning with pleasure, that some parents adopt a better plan; and that some young ladies, even thus educated, have had understanding enough to lay aside the greatest part of the abovemen- tioned frippery, and cultivate such knowledge, and such virtues, as were ornamental to society, and useful to themselves.

Such, with a few trifling variations, is the common course of European [including British] education; a course, which seems almost entirely cal- culated to cultivate the personal graces, while the care of the head and of the heart, is little, if at all, attended to; and the useful duties of domestic life, but too often turned into ridicule. (47–49)

HESTER CHAPONE

Hester Chapone was one of many eighteenth-century women who prescribed a specific curriculum for the education of young ladies. Each of these writers had a plan of her own, sometimes becoming so specific as to suggest which authors were fit for a young lady to read and which ones were not. Most presented plans that addressed morality and spirituality as well as practicality, fashionability, and (sometimes only as an afterthought) intellectual activity. Chapone's essay is conservative in tone, following Rousseau's recommendation that girls be taught what will be of most use to them as adult women. A lady's first obligation in her role as a wife and mother, according to Chapone, is "economy," which in the eighteenth century was understood to mean more than mere financial wisdom. The term *economy* encompassed the whole range of what late twentieth-century readers would think of as home economics or effective household management. The first excerpt from Chapone's essay defines what she sees as the importance of this kind of economy for women.

In addition to advising young women about the economics of homemaking, Chapone also suggests which accomplishments to pursue and to what extent it is advisable to pursue each of them. She warns about placing too much importance on mere ornamental accomplishments, though she recognizes that such accomplishments can be both useful and enjoyable. She also warns against too much intellectual development, believing that a scholarly woman is less womanly than one who has only a modicum of knowledge about intellectual subjects.

Chapone's ideas about what is and what is not proper and beneficial for a young woman to study are similar to those of many other writers of her day. Her attitude seems to be that anything that does not strain a woman's intellect, make a woman competitive with a man, damage her health, cause her to form strong opinions of her own, or cause her to appear to be less than respectable is fine—as long as her "best friends," a term generally applied to her parents and other respected and mature advisors, accede to it. Most conduct book writers of the day, both conservative and liberal, advised women to consult their parents, guardians, and other mature, respectable friends before making decisions that could have an impact on their futures. Young women were regularly told to consult such friends before making decisions ranging from which books to read and what dresses to wear to when and whom they should marry.

FROM HESTER CHAPONE, *ON THE IMPROVEMENT OF THE MIND*
(1770?)

Economy is so important a part of a woman's character, so necessary to her own happiness, and so essential to her performing properly the duties of a wife and of a mother, that it ought to have the precedence of all other accomplishments, and take its rank next to the first duties of life. It is, moreover, an art as well as a virtue; and many well-meaning persons, from ignorance, or from inconsideration, are strangely deficient in it. Indeed, it is too often wholly neglected in a young woman's education; and she is sent from her father's house to govern a family, without the least degree of that knowledge which should qualify her for it: this is the source of much inconvenience, for, though experience and attention may supply, by degrees, the want of instruction, yet this requires time: the family, in the mean time, may get into habits which are very difficult to alter; and, what is worse, the husband's opinion of his wife's incapacity may be fixed too strongly to suffer him ever to think justly of her gradual improvements. I would, therefore, earnestly advise you to make use of every opportunity you can find, for laying in some store of knowledge on this subject, before you are called upon to the practice; by observing what passes before you, by consulting prudent and experienced mistresses of families, and by entering in a book a memorandum of every new piece of intelligence you acquire: you may afterward compare these with more mature observations, and you can make additions and corrections as you see occasion. (88–89)

• • •

With regard to accomplishments, the chief of these is a competent share of reading, well chosen and properly regulated. . . . Dancing, and the knowledge of the French tongue, are now so universal, that they cannot be dispensed with in the education of a gentlewoman; and indeed, they are both useful as well as ornamental: the first by forming and strengthening the body, and improving the carriage; the second, by opening a large field of entertainment and improvement for the mind. I believe there are more agreeable books of female literature in French than in any other language: and, as they are not less commonly talked of than English books, you must often feel mortified in company, if you are too ignorant to read them. . . .

To write a free and legible hand, and to understand common arithmetic, are indispensable requisites.

As to music and drawing, I would only wish you to follow as genius [innate ability] leads. . . . I think the use of both these arts is more for yourself than others. It is but seldom that a private person has leisure or application enough to gain any high degree of excellence in them; and your own partial family are perhaps the only persons who would not much rather be entertained by the performance of a professor [professional performer or teacher] than by yours: but with regard to yourself, it is of great consequence to have the power of filling up agreeably those intervals of time which too often hang heavily on the hands of a woman, if her lot be cast in a retired situation. . . .

As to the learned languages [Latin and Greek], though I respect the abilities and application of those ladies who have obtained them, and who make a modest and proper use of them. Yet I would by no means advise you, or any other woman, who is not strongly impelled by a particular genius, to engage in such studies. The labour and time which they require are generally incompatible with our natures and proper employments: the real knowledge which they supply, is not essential, since the English, French, or Italian tongues afford tolerable translations of all the most valuable productions of antiquity, besides the multitude of original authors which they furnish; and these are much more than sufficient to store your mind with as many ideas as you will know how to manage. The danger of pedantry and presumption in a woman—of her exciting envy in one sex, and jealousy in the other—of her exchanging the graces of imagination for the severity and preciseness of a scholar, would be, I own, sufficient to frighten me from the ambition of seeing my girl remarkable for learning. Such objections are, perhaps, still stronger with regard to the abstruse sciences.

Whatever tends to embellish your fancy, to enlighten your understanding, and furnish you with ideas to reflect upon when alone, or to converse upon in company, is certainly well worth your acquisition. The wretched expedient, to which ignorance so often drives our sex, of calling in slander to enliven the tedious insipidity of conversation, would alone be a strong reason for enriching your mind with innocent subjects of entertainments, which may render you a fit companion for persons of sense and knowledge, from whom you may reap the most desirable improvements: for, though I think reading indispensably necessary to the due cultivation of your mind, I prefer the conversation of such persons to every other method of instruction; but this you cannot hope to enjoy, unless you qualify yourself to bear a part in such society, by, at least, a moderate share of reading.

Though *religion* is the most important of all your pursuits, there are not many books on that subject which I should recommend to you at present. Controversy is wholly improper at your age. . . .

The principal study I would recommend is *history*. I know of nothing equally proper to entertain and improve at the same time, or that is so likely to form and strengthen your judgement, and, by giving you a liberal and comprehensive view of human nature, in some measure to supply the defect of that experience, which is usually attained too late to be of much service to us. Let me add, that more materials for conversations are supplied by this kind of knowledge than by almost any other. . . .

The faculty in which women usually most excell is that of imagination; and when properly cultivated, it becomes the source of all that is most charming in society. Nothing you can read will so much contribute to the improvement of this faculty as *poetry*; which, if applied to its true ends, adds a thousand charms to those sentiments of religion, virtue, generosity, and delicate tenderness, by which the human soul is exalted and refined. I hope you are not deficient in natural taste for this enchanting art, but that you will find it one of your greatest pleasures to be conversant with the best poets, whom our language can bring you acquainted with, particularly those immortal ornaments of our nation, Shakespeare and Milton. . . .

Natural Philosophy, in the largest sense of the expression, is too wide a field for you to undertake: but the study of nature, as far as may suit your powers and opportunities, you will find a most sublime entertainment: the objects of this study are all the stupendous works of the Almighty Hand, that lie within the reach of our observation. In the works of man, perfection is aimed at; but it can only be found in those of the Creator. The contemplation of perfection must produce delight, and every natural object around you would offer this delight, if it could attract your attention. . . .

Moral Philosophy, as it relates to human actions, is of still higher importance than the study of nature. The works of the ancients on this subject are universally said to be entertaining as well as instructive, by those who can read them in their original languages; and such of them as are well translated, will, undoubtedly, some years hence, afford you great pleasure and improvement. You will also find many agreeable and useful books, written originally in French and English, on morals and manners: for the present, there are works, which, without assuming the solemn air of philosophy, will enlighten your mind on these subjects, and intrude instruction in an easier dress; of this sort are many of the moral essays that have appeared in periodical papers; which, when excellent in their kind—as are the Spectators, Guardians, Ramblers, and Adventurers—are particularly useful to young people, as they comprehend a great variety of subjects, introduce many ideas and observations that are new to them,—and lead to a habit of reflecting on the characters and events that come before them in real life, which I consider as the best exercise of the understanding. . . .

I would by no means exclude the kind of reading which young people are naturally the most fond of: though I think the greatest care should be taken in the choice of those fictitious stories, that so enchant the mind; most of which tend to inflame the passions of youth, whilst the chief purpose of education should be to moderate and restrain them. Add to this, that both the writing and sentiments of most novels and romances are such as are only proper to vitiate your style, and to mislead your heart and understanding. The expectation of extraordinary adventures, which seldom ever happen to the sober and prudent part of mankind, and the admiration of extravagant passions and absurd conduct, are some of the usual fruits of this kind of reasoning; which, when a young woman makes it her chief amusement, generally render her ridiculous in conversation, and miserably wrongheaded in her pursuits and behaviour. There are, however, works of this class, in which excellent morality is joined with the most lively pictures of the human mind, and with all that can entertain the imagination and interest the heart. But I must repeatedly exhort you, never to read any thing of the sentimental kind, without taking the judgment of your best friends in the choice: for, I am persuaded, that the indiscriminate reading of such kind of books corrupts more female hearts than any other cause whatsoever. (109–113, 116–119)

Source: Hester Chapone, Dr. John Gregory, and Lady Sarah Pennington, *Chapone's Improvement of the Mind; Gregory's Legacy; Lady Pennington's Advice* (London: Scott and Webster, n.d.).

LADY SARAH PENNINGTON

Lady Pennington was separated from her husband, by his demand and through no apparent fault of her own. Because under English law in the eighteenth century children were legally treated as the property of the husband, her daughters remained with Lord Pennington. Lady Pennington was not allowed to raise them or even to communicate with them directly. Nonetheless, she felt an obligation to guide them as a mother is expected to do. As noted in Chapter 3, she published a lengthy essay, hoping that her daughters (as well as other young women) would read and profit from it. One part of the essay treats the issue of a proper education for young women of their standing in society.

Lady Pennington's advice resembles Chapone's in many ways, but her tone and emphasis differ. She places much greater trust in the judgment of young women, especially in regard to spiritual and intellectual pursuits, than does Chapone, and is much more supportive of young women following their intellectual interests. Nevertheless, Lady Pennington points out the need for a woman to remember her inferiority to men in matters of intellect. Pennington's view is that this inferiority springs from "the difference in education" of men and women, not from inherent differences in the sexes, but she does not rail against such differences in education. Instead she suggests that the fact of her inferiority will keep the woman "humble" and will be "an effectual check" on a tendency toward overtalkativeness.

Like Chapone and most other writers of the period, Pennington observes that a woman's first duty is to her "proper sphere," the sphere of respectable wifehood and motherhood. Pennington's view is that a woman can reasonably and appropriately pursue some intellectual ideas (including those involving the controversies of religion through study of scriptures and other spiritual writings), but that she should never allow those studies to stand in the way of adhering to society's expectations of her as a wife and mother.

FROM LADY SARAH PENNINGTON, *AN UNFORTUNATE MOTHER'S ADVICE TO HER ABSENT DAUGHTERS* (1761)

One half hour, or more, either before, or immediately after breakfast, I would have you constantly give to the attentive perusal of some rationally pious author, or some part of the New Testament, with which, and indeed with the whole Scripture, you ought to make yourself perfectly acquainted, as the basis on which your religion is founded. From this practice you will reap more real benefit than can be supposed by those who have never made the experiment. The other hours may be divided amongst those necessary and polite acquisitions, which are suitable to your sex, age, and to your rank in life.—Study your own language thoroughly, that you may speak correctly, and write grammatically;—do not content yourself with the common use of words which custom has taught you from the cradle, but learn from whence they are derived, and what are their proper significations. French you ought to be as well acquainted with as with English: and Italian might, without much difficulty, be added. Acquire a good knowledge of history—that of your own country first, then of the other European nations—read them not with a view to amuse, but to improve your mind—and to that end, make reflections on what you have read, which may be useful to yourself, and will render your conversation agreeable to others. Learn so much of geography, as to form a just idea of the situation of places mentioned in any author, and this will make history more entertaining to you.

It is necessary for you to be perfect in the four first rules of arithmetic: more you can never have occasion for, and the mind should not be burdened with needless application. Music and drawing are accomplishments well worth the trouble of attaining, if your inclination and genius lead to either; if not, do not attempt them, for it will be only much time and great labor unprofitably thrown away, it being next to impossible to arrive at any degree of perfection in those arts, by the dint of perseverance only, if a good ear and a native genius be wanting. The study of natural philosophy you will find both pleasing and instructive—pleasing, from the continual new discoveries to be made of the innumerably various beauties of nature—a most agreeable gratification of that desire of knowledge wisely implanted in the human mind—and highly instructive, as those discoveries lead to the contemplation of the great Author of nature, whose wisdom and goodness so conspicuously shine through all his works, that it is impossible to reflect seriously on them without admiration and gratitude.

These, my dear, are but a few of those mental improvements I would recommend to you; indeed there is no branch of knowledge that your capacity is equal to, and which you have an opportunity of acquiring, that, I think, ought to be neglected. It has been objected against all female learning beyond that of household economy, that it tends only to fill the minds of the sex with a conceited vanity, which sets them above their proper business—occasions an indifference to, if not a total neglect of, their family affairs—and serves only to render them useless wives and impertinent companions. It must be confessed, that some reading ladies have given but too much cause for this objection: and, could it be proved to hold good throughout the sex, it would certainly be right to confine their improvements within the narrow limits of the nursery, of the kitchen, and the confectionery; but, I believe it will upon examination, be found, that such ill consequences proceed chiefly from too great an imbecility of mind to be capable of much enlargement, or from a mere affectation of knowledge, void of all reality. Vanity is never the result of understanding; a sensible woman will soon be convinced, that all the learning her utmost application can make her mistress of, will be, from the difference of education, in many points inferior to that of a school-boy; this reflection will keep her always humble, and will be an effectual check to that loquacity, which renders some women such insupportable companions.

The management of all domestic affairs is certainly the proper business of women; and, unfashionably rustic as such an assertion may be thought, it is not beneath the dignity of any lady, however high her rank, to know how to educate her children, to govern her servants—how to order an elegant table with economy, and to manage her whole family with prudence, regularity, and method: if in these she is defective, whatever may be her attainments in any other kinds of knowledge, she will act out of character: and by not moving in her proper sphere, she will become rather the object of ridicule than of approbation. (204–206)

Source: Hester Chapone, Dr. John Gregory, and Lady Sarah Pennington, *Chapone's Improvement of the Mind; Gregory's Legacy; Lady Pennington's Advice* (London: Scott and Webster, n.d.).

JANE WEST

In her three-volume work on "the duties and character of women," Jane West makes many recommendations about the education of the young woman in English society. Like Alexander, Chapone, and Pennington, West believes that the trends toward "fashionable" education of women in the eighteenth century are filled with dangers. Such an education, as she sees it, is in fact miseducation.

West's fear about the dangers of fashionable life in a world that seems to be becoming more dissolute and less attentive to respectability and high ethical standards than it was in her own childhood is clear in the first excerpt from her *Letters to a Young Lady*. Her remedy for the problem is a specific educational regimen founded on the study of Christian principles and practice. Unlike Chapone, who disapproves of educating young women in the "controversies" of Christianity, West believes that not inculcating clearly defined Christian doctrine and principles at an early age is tantamount to leaving the child unprotected from the immoral influences she will inevitably confront at various times throughout her life.

The necessity of religious instruction cannot, according to Jane West, be overemphasized. The focus on science and non-Christian philosophy that had overtaken so much of educational theory in the late eighteenth century and the early nineteenth century made training in Christian doctrine, principle, and scripture even more imperative than previously.

Jane West concerned herself with many aspects of the education of young women of quality. No area, however, was as important to her as spiritual training. West did not believe in protecting young women from contemporary ideas about science by keeping them ignorant. Instead, she believed that any young woman who was taught Christian doctrine and principle properly and thoroughly would be competent to judge scientific education appropriately, believing what fit in with scriptural revelation and remaining skeptical of the rest. Unlike Hester Chapone, West trusted that a young woman's ability to reason properly would enable her to determine the truth or falsity of religious controversies. She believed that spiritual ignorance was a much greater danger to the girl and woman than knowledge of spiritual controversies.

FROM JANE WEST, *LETTERS TO A YOUNG LADY, IN WHICH THE DUTIES AND CHARACTER OF WOMEN ARE CONSIDERED* (London, 1806, 2nd ed., 3 vols.)

The society, which young women who are devoted to a life of fashionable amusement frequently meet, creates a species of danger which in the present times is most truly alarming. The unblushing effrontery with which women of doubtful or lost character obtrude themselves upon public notice, is a marked characteristic of the age we live in, that was unknown to our ancestors . . . and strongly demonstrative that the outposts of female honour are given up. What can more tend to debase the purity of virtue, and to enfeeble the stability of principle, than to find that a notorious courtesan retains all the distinctions due to unspotted chastity; nay, even to see her pointed out as a most engaging creature, with a truly benevolent heart; while all retrospect of her flagit[i]ous conduct is prevented, by the observation, that we have nothing to do with people's private character. Can we wonder, that, since the age is become so liberal, profligacy should not feel the necessity of being *guarded* in its transgressions? . . .

Nor are the evils consequent on a life of dissipation the only dangers that young ladies may now dread. In retirement, they are haunted by another species of enemies, no less alarming to their understandings, to their morals, and to their repose. The species of reading, prepared to relieve the toils of dissipation, is faithful to its interests, and is either intended to mislead or to gratify. Under the former description may be ranked all those systems of ethics, and treatises on education, which are founded on the false doctrine of human perfectibility, and consequently reject the necessity of divine revelation and supernatural agency. Many elementary works on the sciences come under this description; and by these the young student may learn that she is a free independent being, endowed with energies which she may exert at will, and restrained by no considerations but those which her own judgment may think it *expedient* to obey. She is taught, that the nature she inherits was originally perfect; that its present disordered state did not arise from an hereditary taint, the consequence of primeval rebellion, but from wretched systems of worldly policy, ill conceived laws, and illiberal restraints; which if happily removed, the human mind would at once start forth in a rapid pursuit of that perfection which it is fully able to attain. She will hear much praise bestowed on generosity, greatness of soul, liberality, benevolence, and this cast of virtues; but as their offices and properties would not be clearly defined, and as all reference to the preventing and assisting grace of God, or to the clear explanations which accompany Christian ethics, are systematically excluded from these compositions, it will not be wonderful if the bewildered reader should bestow these titles to the actions of pride, pertinacity, indiscretion, and extravagance. We have seen the effects of these theories on the vacant impetuous mind of uninstructed youth, sufficiently to determine, that, like the pagan corrupters of old time, who "changed the glory of the invisible God into an image made like unto corruptible man," they, while "professing themselves to be wise, have become fools."

But we will suppose a young woman happily free from the metaphysical mania, and influenced by no inordinate desire to distinguish herself among her companions by the disgusting affectation of superior knowledge; I mean by this, a common character, who is willing to slide with the world; who reads to kill time; who adopts the opinions that she hears, and suffers the passing scene to flit by her without much anxiety, or much reflection. Unengaging as this character is, I confess that I greatly prefer it to the petticoat philosophist, who seeks for eminence and distinction in infidelity and skepticism, or in the equally monstrous extravagances of German morality. Women of ordinary abilities were in former times confined to their samplers or their confectionery; and surely they were as well employed in picking out the seeds of currants, or in stitching the "tale of Troy divine," as now, when they are dependant on the circulating library for means to overcome the tedium of a *disengaged* day.

Novels, plays, and perhaps a little poetry, are the limits of their literary researches. Shall we inquire what impressions romantic adventures, high-wrought scenes of passion, and all the turmoil of intrigue, incident, extravagant attachment, and improbable vicissitudes of fortune, must make upon a vacant mind, whose judgment has not been exercised either by real information, or the conclusions of experience and observation? The inferences that we *must* draw are self-evident. . . .

We may inquire, how are women fitted to answer those severe demands which custom, and I may add reason, make upon their conduct? This investigation will lead us into an ample field; as it will not only require us to consider what education does in forming habits of watchfulness and self-control, and in invigorating the discriminative and deliberative powers of the mind; but also, how far the present customs of society assist us in the proper discharge of our required duties. In the course of this inquiry, we shall discover ample reason to bless our Creator, who originally intended us to "take our noiseless Way along the cool sequestered vale of life," since we shall find every departure from this appointed path attended with danger, either to our peace, or to our renown. (Vol. 1, 10–28)

· · ·

It being the first business of education to prepare the mind for that warfare with our spiritual enemies which will never finally terminate on this side the grave, and in which the christian, though sometimes overpowered, must ever rise with renewed hope to overcome; let us, above all things, endeavour to equip the destined combatants "in the whole armour of God." Let us give them not only a thorough knowledge of their duty, but carefully exercise them in the *practice* of it; teaching them to act always upon christian *principles*, and to view every event through christian *optics*. This cannot be done, unless we make them intimately conversant with the truths of revelation; and surely no language can be so proper as that which the Spirit of God employed to instruct mankind, and of which we possess a sufficiently faithful translation in our English Scriptures. Let me strongly urge every mother to make her children adepts in both the Old and New Testaments. Merely reading them is not sufficient; they should be taught to reflect and converse upon sacred subjects, as the only way of clearly understanding what they peruse. By the use of bibles with marginal references, she may accustom them to illustrate precepts by facts, and to connect facts with precepts; the type and its antetype may be shown together, the prophecy and its fulfilment, the promise and its accomplishment, the threatening and the chastisement. Let her show them the vast superiority of sacred over profane history, not merely on account of its indubitable verity, or from its being the *oldest* authentic record of past ages, but because every fact that it contains is expressly said to be written for our instruction. The method by which God saw fit to make himself known to mankind was by historical narrative; this being the least subject to imposture or misrepresentation, carrying with it the strongest evidence, and therefore being best suited to convince every understanding, and to impress its authority upon every age, from that which witnessed the event to the last records of time. Let not the minds of children, therefore, be suffered to rest in the mere circumstances of the narrative[s] they are perusing, beautiful and impressive as they often are; but, as soon as their unfolding faculties will permit, open their minds to the *great designs* of God's providence, which the incidental sufferings or exaltation of good and bad men alternately furthered. It was not for his personal virtue, much less from partial affection, that Jacob was chosen to be the father of the promised see, and Esau prohibited from receiving the blessing. Josiah was not slain in punishment for his sins, nor Jeroboam exalted over the degenerate house of David in consideration of his superior merit. . . .

Nothing is so apt to embarrass young minds, and to unsettle their faith and trust in God, as the apparently unequal dispensations of Providence, in often giving success to vice, and allotting afflictions to virtue. Temporal prosperity is now almost universally held out as the reward of desert, in those fictitious histories on which youth are too much made to depend for moral instruction; can we then wonder that dispassionate observers should lament that success is universally considered as the criterion of merit? A thorough acquaintance with the book of God will teach children to estimate human actions and human affairs by *juster* principles, and induce them to consider every instance of unequal distribution for which they cannot account, as an irrefragable confirmation of the certainty of a future state. (Vol. 3, 269–274)

• • •

Religious instruction . . . is of a twofold nature. It should be commenced early, not to instill prejudice, but to guard against prepossessions, and to impress the learner's mind with a proper conviction of the importance of the work. This instruction must be ever suited to the age and understanding of the pupil, both in matter and degree; but when the girl writes woman, let the mother deeply impress upon her daughter's mind this solemn consideration, that as religion discloses to us another world, in which the employment of the blessed, during the circling years of eternity, will be to know and to adore God, if we would enjoy the promised heaven, we must in this life cultivate those habits. For the soul carries with it the propensities that it acquired below; and how shall we become meet for the society of angels, if we neither understand nor delight in their occupations?

The scientifical turn which education has lately taken, increases the necessity for early imbuing the juvenile mind with a sense of the divine authority of scripture, and of the insufficiency of human reason to discover the origin and end of man. Women are seldom very deeply versed in any branch of philosophy; and a smattering of science is extremely apt to generate that dependence upon second causes, which is one of the strong-holds of deism in weak minds. A half-informed young woman, when she has found out the *immediate* reason of vegetation, congelation, or any elementary process, is too apt to think that she has discovered *all*, without extending her views to the great God who at first endowed matter with those wonderful properties which it has possessed for many thousand years, and without whose continual influence every moment in the stupendous machine of nature would become confused and disordered. The danger of the young student's views being thus limited, is increased by the prevalent use of terms, adopted, perhaps, from a persuasion that they are comprehensive, but which an eminent scholar and divine [Dr. Paley] proves to be unphilosophical; such as "the power of attraction, the law of vegetation, the order of the seasons," and the like. "Inert matter," he observes, "has no power; a law pre-supposes a law-giver; and a propelling impetus must originate in something foreign to the thing thus over-ruled." Were we sure that these studies would be extended till mind obtained that link in the chain of science, which proves the necessary dependance of material nature on intellectual existence, we should be certain of gaining a sincere, though late convert to revealed truth; but when we consider how soon the progress of learning will be arrested by the frivolous pursuits or business of life, let us at least take care to run no hazard of unfitting the mind for the reception of what it is most necessary it should know.

I have taken for granted, that the books selected for the purpose of scientific instruction, though they may not . . . be purposely designed to lead the reader from nature to nature's God, have yet no covert intention of perverting the mind which they pretend to inform. But this is granting more than the generality of elementary tracts on the sciences will warrant: A respectable writer has clearly ascertained, by her highly judicious and salutary (though, to herself, irksome) investigation, that a *settled* design to overturn the established faith of this country, and to illuminize the minds of the rising generation, are the chief motives of the multifarious books for the education of youth which have deluged the nation. In this design of fitting the rising hope of Britain for a pandemonium of philosophists, no branch of information has been suffered to escape untainted. If the young lady read history, she will find it questioned whether the propagation of the gospel really was accomplished by miracles or by human ingenuity; whether the early christians were martyrs or fanatics; and whether much good has resulted from the extension of the religion of Jesus? In the biographical sketches, she will find piety, or at least attachment to any peculiar mode of worship, coupled with a weak understanding, or a contracted heart; while heathen persecutors, deists, and libertines, are adorned with the freshest flowers of eulogy. If she read geography, or travels, she will perceive it doubted, or perhaps denied, that the earth is of the age which the Mosaical chronology affirms, or that the events recorded in holy writ could have taken place in countries which it describes in such different colours from their present state. In natural history, she will find cavils against the miracles recorded in scripture; sarcasms on the histories of Balaam, Jonah, and the prophet of Judah, will be obtruded into descriptions of the natural properties of the ass, the whale, and the lion; and perhaps the wonderful preservation of the three pious captives from the rage of Nebuchadnezzar, may *humorously* illustrate the fable of the salamander. In chemistry and mineralogy, she will be informed of the astonishing effects that various combinations of ingredients, mechanical contrivances, and geometrical properties, can produce; and she will be reminded, that when natural preparations can assume appearances seemingly miraculous, we should scruple to call in an invisible agent. Some instances will be given of successful cheats; and it will then be asked, with much apparent modesty, if the flowering rod of Aaron might not have been a slight [*sic*] of hand illusion, and the cures of Christ have proceeded from a degree of medicinal knowledge unknown in a barbarous country? Astronomy also supplies a very powerful engine for shaking the faith of those who expected scripture to develop the secrets of nature, instead of the mysteries of grace; and that the inspired narrator of the creation, should have prematurely disclosed the laws of planetary motion, to gratify the curious; when his mission was intended to preserve, in one nation, a sense of the obligation to worship the "Lord God, who fashioned the earth and all things that are therein," who made the heavens and all their host, who sanctified the closing day of creation, and who suspended the punishment of disobedient man, and again set life and death before him.

When a young woman has been duly informed that scripture narration is designed to illustrate moral and theological truths, she will not reject it because its language is accommodated to the prevailing ideas of the times in which it was written. She well knows, that "the pillars of the round world," must be metaphorically understood, and that the rotation of the sun round the earth is a condescension to popular opinion. She will confess that the existence of deceit is no argument against the reality of truth; and she will make herself mistress of the different criteria by which true and false miracles are distinguished. She will see, that natural properties are no restraint on the possible interposition of the supernatural Power who bestowed them; and that if the Deity visibly interposes, he must act by miracle. She will allow, that a difference in government and cultivation will change the natural aspect of countries; and she will pay little respect to the pretended data of the high antiquity of the earth, when she perceives that the alleged facts are controverted, and that no two geologists draw the same inferences from the same analysis. Lastly, she will not feel her faith shaken by the partial observations of infidel historians, or sceptical biographers; but will pity the situation of those who are resolutely bent to mis state and mislead. Their futile spleen will only serve to confirm her faith; for she must recollect her Lord's prediction, "that the world would say all manner of evil, *falsely*, of his disciples, for his name's sake." (Vol. 1, 358–368)

CATHERINE MACAULAY GRAHAM

Most writers on educational theory and practice in late eighteenth- and early nineteenth-century England concentrated on the biological and social differences of men and women, and how those differences dictated different kinds of education. Catherine Macaulay was an exception to this rule. In her 1790 *Letters on Education*, she suggested that equality of education between boys and girls would lead to intellectual equality between men and women, a result that she believed would greatly benefit society as a whole as well as the individuals within that society. Ancient societies may have had good reasons for separating the sexes educationally, she asserts, but modern society can only suffer as a result of following that example.

Macaulay's ideal of education and of society requires equality between the sexes. She proposes a society in which men and women are encouraged to learn to the best of their capacity and to hold positions in the world and in the family that best suit their needs and desires as individuals, as family members, and as citizens.

Macaulay's views were considered radical in their time. Many people dismissed her ideas as the ravings of a "masculine woman," a phrase denoting something "unnatural" to the populace. Her ideas were disseminated widely, however, and although they received little respect at the time, they eventually began to have some influence. As a result of the writings of "unnatural" women like

Macaulay and Wollstonecraft, the idea of equal education for both sexes began to become a serious part of the dialogue regarding educational theory. It was not until the beginning of the twentieth century that women could receive an education in the academic community equal in quality to that available to men. Nevertheless, Macaulay's treatise laid significant groundwork for the movement toward equality of the sexes in education.

FROM CATHERINE MACAULAY GRAHAM, *LETTERS ON EDUCATION WITH OBSERVATIONS ON RELIGIOUS AND METAPHYSICAL SUBJECTS*
(London, 1790)

The moderns, in the education of their children, have too much followed the stiff and prudish manners of ancient days, in separating the male and female children of a family. This is well adapted to the absurd unsocial rigour of Grecian manners; but as it is not so agreeable to that mixture of the sexes in a more advanced age, which prevails in all European societies, it is not easy to be accounted for, but from the absurd notion, that the education of females should be of an opposite kind to that of males. How many nervous diseases have been contracted? How much feebleness of constitution has been acquired, by forming a false idea of female excellence, and endeavouring, by our art, to bring Nature to the play of our imagination. Our sons are suffered to enjoy with freedom that time which is not devoted to study, and may follow, unmolested, those strong impulses which Nature has wisely given for the furtherance of her benevolent purposes; but if, before her natural vivacity is entirely subdued by habit, little Miss is inclined to show her locomotive tricks in a manner not entirely agreeable to the trammels of custom, she is reproved with a sharpness which gives her a consciousness of having highly transgressed the laws of decorum; and what with the vigilance of those who are appointed to superintend her conduct, and the false biass they have imposed on her mind, every vigorous exertion is suppressed, the mind and body yield to the tyranny of error, and Nature is charged with all those imperfections which we alone owe to the blunders of art.

I could say a great deal . . . on those personal advantages, which the strength of the mother gives to her offspring, and the ill effects which must accrue both to the male and female issue from her feebleness. I could expatiate on the mental advantages which accompany a firm constitution, and on that evenness and complacency of temper, which commonly attends the blessing health. I could turn the other side of the arguments, and show you, that most of the caprices, the teasing follies, and often the vices of women, proceed from weakness, or some other defect in their corporeal frame; but when I have sifted the subject to the bottom, and taken every necessary trouble to illustrate and enforce my opinion, I shall, perhaps, still continue singular in it. My arguments may serve only to strengthen my ideas, and my sex will continue to lisp with their tongues, to totter in their walk, and to counterfeit more weakness and sickness than they really have, in order to attract the notice of the male; for, says a very elegant author [Edmund Burke], perfection is not the proper object of love: we admire excellence, but we are more inclined to love those we despise.

There is another prejudice . . . which affects yet more deeply female happiness, and female importance; a prejudice, which ought ever to have been confined to the regions of the east, [a] state of slavery to which female nature in that part of the world has been ever subjected, and can only suit with the notion of a positive inferiority in the intellectual powers of the female mind. You will soon perceive, that the prejudice which I mean, is that degrading difference in the culture of the understanding, which has prevailed for several centuries in all European societies. Our ancestors, on the first revival of letters, dispensed with an equal hand the advantages of a classical education to all their offspring; but as pedantry was the fault of that age, a female student might not at that time be a very agreeable character. True philosophy in those ages was rarely an attendant on learning, even in the male sex; but it must be obvious to all those who are blinded by the mist of prejudice, that there is no cultivation of the understanding; and that a mind, irradiated by the clear light of wisdom, must be equal to every task which reason imposes on it. The social duties in the interesting characters of daughter, wife, and mother, will be but ill performed by ignorance and levity; and in the domestic converse of husband and wife, the alternative of an enlightened, or an unenlightened companion, cannot be indifferent to any man of taste and true knowledge. Be no longer niggards, then, O ye parents, in bestowing on your offspring, every blessing which nature and fortune renders them capable of enjoying! Confine not the education of your daughters to what is regarded as the ornamental parts of it, nor deny the graces to your sons. Suffer no prejudices to prevail on you to weaken Nature, in order to render her more beautiful; take measures for the virtue and the harmony of your family, by uniting their young minds early in the soft bonds of friendship. Let your children be brought up together; let their sports and studies be the same; let them enjoy, in the constant presence of those who are set over them, all that freedom which innocence renders harmless, and in which Nature rejoices. By the uninterrupted intercourse which you will thus establish, both sexes will find, that friendship may be enjoyed between them without passion. The wisdom of your daughters will preserve them from the bane of coquetry, and even at the age of desire, objects of temptation will lose somewhat of their stimuli, by losing their novelty. Your sons will look for something more solid in women, than a mere outside; and be no longer the dupes to the meanest, the weakest, and the most profligate of the sex. They will become the constant benefactors of that part of their family who stand in need of their assistance; and in regard to all matters of domestic concern, the unjust distinction of primogeniture will be deprived of its sting. (46–50)

The education of women was a subject open to much debate in Austen's time. Works like Rousseau's *Emile* and John Locke's *Some Thoughts Concerning Education* dealt primarily with theories of educating boys into men, particularly among the gentry and aristocracy (Book Five of *Emile* does, however, provide specific reasons why girls' education should be different from boys' in most ways). Works such as Gregory's, Chapone's, Pennington's, and West's opened a wider and more specific discussion of education for women, advocating curricula that would best prepare the young woman for the role in life that each author considered proper. Macaulay, along with other writers of the early women's movement, advocated equal education along with greater opportunity for women to fill a greater variety of roles, both in the home and in society. Regardless of the role each writer believed that women should fill, the most conservative to the most liberal considered education the key to preparing women appropriately and adequately.

Figure 5.1. Professional portrait of Jane Austen. *Source:* Hubbard, Elbert. *Little Journeys to the Homes of Famous Women*. New York: Putnam's Sons, 1897, plate following page 324.

CHAWTON COTTAGE FROM THE ROAD.

Figure 5.2. Chawton Cottage, home of Jane Austen, her sister Cassandra, and their mother. *Source:* Adams, Oscar Fay. *The Story of Jane Austen's Life.* New ed. Boston: Lee and Shepard, 1897, 145.

TOPICS FOR WRITTEN OR ORAL EXPLORATION

1. Consider the following girls and women in terms of their characters, their intellects, and their attitudes: Mrs. Bennet, Elizabeth Bennet, Jane Bennet, Lydia Bennet, Mary Bennet, Miss Bingley, Charlotte Lucas, Georgiana Darcy, Lady Catherine de Bourgh, Anne de Bourgh. Then decide which of the methods of instruction outlined in the documents presented in this chapter each character seems most likely to have experienced, and why. Choose two of these characters and write an essay in which you analyze how such an education might create some- one with the attitudes and ideas of the women you have chosen.

2. For each writer represented in this chapter, determine which of their ideas seem to agree with Austen's ideas about appropriate education for women, and which don't. Choose one author and write an essay in which you discuss to what extent Austen's novel seems to support or refute his or her ideas about educating girls and women.

3. Most formal education (and even most informal education) in Austen's time was conducted in a single-sex atmosphere. Today, most formal education takes place in mixed-gender settings. Which environment do you believe contributes more to the intellectual development of students, single-sex schools or mixed-gender schools? Is being in a single-sex school of greater advantage to boys than to girls, to girls than to boys, or equivalent in terms of advantages? After a discussion of some of the issues involved, divide the class into two groups: one in favor of single-sex schools, and one preferring mixed-gender schools (if there is not a relatively even number of students on each side, some may need to be assigned to argue for the view they do not support). Provide time for the teams to plan their strategy. Then stage a debate on the advantages and disadvantages of single-sex and mixed-gender schools in our time.

4. In Austen's time, issues of morality and spirituality were considered to be important components of education. Today there is much debate over whether schools should "teach" morality and values. In the United States, the separation of church and state prevents explicit re- ligious teaching in the public schools. What place do you believe that morality, values, and religion should have in a student's educational life? Discuss the consequences, both positive and negative, of incor- porating religion and morality into the curriculum of the public schools.

5. Divide the class into groups of three to four people. Then begin to draft a document that represents a consensus of what you, as a group, believe the education of a young person should consist of at the pres-

ent time. Be sure to consider such factors as the need for general knowledge, skills needed to become a valuable worker in the future, and the kind of citizen you want to create through education. Remember that the educational curriculum (the material to be learned) and format (tutorial study, single-sex schools, mixed-gender schools, private school, home study, etc.) you choose will indicate your own educational philosophy and that of the group of which you are a member.

6. After sharing the documents created in the above assignment with the rest of the class, discuss the feasibility of implementing the philosophy or system presented in each document, the strengths and weaknesses of each, and how close your own education comes to the ideal education that you have envisioned in your documents.

7. After reading the documents in this chapter, determine which of the educational programs for young women you believe has the most merit. Discuss whether there are any aspects of that program that continue to be a part of our formal educational process and whether we handle them more or less effectively today than in Austen's time.

8. Based on the values advocated in *Pride and Prejudice*, as well as the novel's comments on education, draft a document that expresses what you believe to be Jane Austen's educational philosophy, especially for women (you may include men as well if you wish). Be able to defend each point of the philosophy with at least one specific incident, idea, or narrator's comment from the novel.

9. Interview a relative or friend who is at least thirty years older than yourself. Ask the individual to discuss his or her experiences with formal education. Once you have gathered the information in the form of an interview, write an analytical essay comparing that person's educational experiences with your own. In your analysis, be sure to take into account changes that have taken place in the world over the last thirty years.

SUGGESTED READINGS

Alexander, William. *The History of Women from the Earliest Antiquity, to the Present Time*. 2 vols. London: W. Strahan and T. Cadell, 1779.

Bennett, John. *Letters to a Young Lady on a Variety of Useful and Interesting Subjects*. 2 vols. London, 1795.

Browne, Alice. *The Eighteenth Century Feminist Mind*. Detroit: Wayne State University Press, 1987.

Chapone's Improvement of the Mind; Gregory's Legacy; Lady Penning-

ton's Advice. By Hester Chapone, Dr. John Gregory, and Lady Sarah Pennington. London: Scott and Webster, n.d.

[Duff, William]. *Letters on the Intellectual and Moral Character of Women. On the Station for Which They Are Destined: On the Characters They Are Qualified to Sustain: and On the Duties They Are Required to Discharge, Both in Private and Social Life.* By the Author of "An Essay on Original Genius"; and of "The History of Rhedi, the Hermit of Mount Ararat." Aberdeen, 1807.

Edgeworth, Maria, and Richard Lovell Edgeworth. *Practical Education.* 2 vols. London: J. Johnson, 1798.

Gardiner, Dorothy. *English Girlhood at School: A Study of Women's Education Through Twelve Centuries.* Oxford: Oxford University Press, 1929.

Gisborne, Thomas. *An Enquiry into the Duties of the Female Sex.* 3rd ed. London: T. Cadell, 1798.

Goldberg, Bette P. *Lessons to Be Learned: A Study of Eighteenth Century Didactic Children's Literature.* New York: Lang, 1984.

Gregory, John. *A Father's Legacy to His Daughters.* London: W. Strahan, T. Cadell, W. Creech, 1774.

Jackson, Mary. *Engines of Instruction, Mischief and Magic: Children's Literature in England.* Lincoln: University of Nebraska Press, 1989.

Kamm, Josephine. *Hope Deferred: Girls' Education in English History.* London: Methuen, 1965.

Lawson, John, and Harold Silver. *A Social History of Education in England.* London: Methuen, 1973.

Locke, John. *Some Thoughts Concerning Education.* 5th ed. London, 1705.

Macaulay Graham, Catherine. *Letters on Education with Observations on Religious and Metaphysical Subjects.* London: C. Dilly, 1790.

More, Hannah. *Strictures on the Modern System of Female Education.* London: T. Cadell Jun. and W. Davies, 1799.

Myers, Sylvia H. "Learning, Virtue, and the Term 'Bluestocking.' " *Studies in Eighteenth Century Culture* 15 (1986): 279–88.

The Oeconomy of Female Life. By a Lady. London, 1751.

Pickering, Samuel F., Jr. *John Locke and Children's Books in Eighteenth Century England.* Knoxville: University of Tennessee Press, 1980.

Progress of a Female Mind. By a Lady. London, 1764.

Rousseau, Jean-Jacques. *Emile; or, Education.* London: J. M. Dent and Sons, 1911.

Wakefield, Priscilla. *Reflections on the Present Condition of the Female Sex with Suggestions for Its Improvement.* London: J. Johnson; Darton and Harvey, 1798.

West, [Jane]. *Letters to a Young Lady, in Which the Duties and Character of Women Are Considered*. 3 vols. 2nd ed. London, 1806.

Wollstonecraft, Mary. *Thoughts on the Education of Daughters: With Reflections on Female Conduct, in the More Important Duties of Life*. London, 1787.

6

Pride and Prejudice: Issues in the 1980s and 1990s

Pride and Prejudice is set at the beginning of the Romantic era, approximately two hundred years ago. Yet the issues explored in the text continue to be debated at the end of the twentieth century, and the debate shows no signs of subsiding as we enter the twenty-first century. Most of these issues are discussed in different terms now from what they were in Austen's time, but they continue to be vital to our society's functioning. Among the issues the novel raises are the following:

- the legal requirements and consequences of marriage;
- how to choose a marriage partner and what that choice will mean to a person's life;
- teenage sexuality, along with its moral and practical ramifications;
- whether a woman can live single successfully in a society that puts such a high premium on a woman's relationship to a man; and
- what kinds of education are best suited for helping children grow into the kinds of men and women our culture needs and wants.

Each of these topics is worthy of more exploration and development than is possible here. I encourage students to pursue individual topics in more detail. This chapter, after a brief consideration of the somewhat amazing popularity of Austen's works in the mass media at the end of the twentieth century, begins the discussion.

"AUSTEN MANIA" IN THE LATE TWENTIETH CENTURY

Any observer of popular culture in the 1980s and 1990s has to be aware of the popularity of Austen's works in film and television format. In the 1980s all of Austen's completed novels—*Sense and Sensibility, Pride and Prejudice, Mansfield Park, Emma, Persuasion*, and *Northanger Abbey*—were produced for television by the British Broadcasting Corporation (BBC). Most were televised in the United States by the Public Broadcasting System and watched by large audiences, and made available as well for purchase on home video.

In the 1990s, Austen's popularity has soared. The creation of motion pictures and commercial television adaptations of her works has generated abundant media attention as well as very high profits for the productions themselves. In its December 18, 1995 issue, for instance, *Newsweek* proclaimed in an article titled "Jane Austen Does Lunch" that the "season's hottest star has been dead 178 years, but the great English novelist is all over the screen" (66). *Time* asked in its January 15, 1996 issue, "Sick of Jane Austen Yet?" The article assured us that we shouldn't be, since the Arts and Entertainment cable network planned to unveil the latest impressive entry in the "Austen revival" within the week (66). *New York* magazine noted, also on January 15, 1996, that America was in the throes of "Jane-Mania" (54). And earlier, in the summer of 1995, *The New Yorker* announced, "Clearly, it's Austenmania in filmland this season" (55).

How much of Austen's work has been available in the 1990s? Besides her novels (which have all been in print almost constantly since their first publication), there have been film adaptations in wide release in the United States of *Sense and Sensibility* (adapted by and starring Emma Thompson, a preeminent and popular British actress), *Persuasion*, and *Emma*. All three have had impressive and popular casts and have been quite successful at the box office. (At least two other film/television versions of *Emma* have been reported on in the press, but they have not, as of this writing, seen the light of day.) An updated movie version of *Emma*, titled *Clueless*, was a hit at the box office and has been transformed into a weekly television series that has tremendous popularity among children and young teenagers in particular. The A&E production of *Pride and Prejudice* created more interest than any other cable network–produced miniseries in history. The ratings it drew were high, videotapes of the series have sold very well, and the critical acclaim generated has been of the highest caliber. Books such as Emma Thompson's *The Sense and Sensibility Screenplay and Diaries* and Sue Birtwistle and Susie Conklin's *The Making of Pride and Prejudice* take us behind the scenes of the making of the movie and the miniseries, enabling us to meld our sense of the present and the past as we see some of our favorite contemporary actors fitting themselves into the costumes and attitudes of Austen's time.

Austen is even found on the World Wide Web. Not only are references to her and her works found in relatively stodgy literary research databases and web links where one might expect to find a 100-plus-year-old novelist, but there is even a listserv (Austen-L) dedicated exclusively to the reading and discussion of Jane Austen's works, life, and times. The listserv, which is administered by a faculty member at McGill University in Montreal, while certainly providing some good resource material for scholars, is primarily frequented by fans, individuals from all walks of life who enjoy reading and discussing Austen's works, the films made from them, and the issues raised by them. There are web lists of Jane Austen jokes, and even popular television series of the 1990s, like *Cybill, Jag*, and the daytime drama *One Life to Live*, have engaged in Austenian references and banter that have been part of the contemporary Austen mania.

Why Jane Austen? Why at this time in history? Speculation abounds. Some people insist that the family values of Austen's time are attractive in a time of such turmoil in the family and in society. Some suggest that the lack of violence in her works enables us to relax, enjoy, and even envy the relative peace of life in Austen's time as it is depicted by filmmakers of the late twentieth century. Others, rather than contrasting Austen's time with our own, compare her characters, their dilemmas, and their reactions to them with the ways people respond to similar dilemmas today. These readers and watchers of Jane Austen's stories are those who subscribe to the "the more we change, the more we stay the same" school of thought. If issues concerning marriage, morality, and social expectation were important in Austen's time, and if they continue to be important in our time, these readers would say, then what Jane Austen had to say to her audience nearly two hundred years ago should remain important to the daily lives of her twentieth-century readers as well.

While all of these perspectives of Austen's works have some validity, none seems to explain thoroughly the upsurge in their popularity in the 1990s. Perhaps explaining the phenomenon is not as important as enjoying it. Jane Austen wrote novels that she believed people could enjoy, in large part because they could recognize parts of themselves and others they knew in the characters and situations she created. The current popularity of her works seems to me to be based on the same premise: we can recognize ourselves, those we love, and those we dislike in Austen's novels. We can relate to the situations she describes, even if the details have changed over time. And yes, we can, while we read her books or watch films made from them, forget about the physical dangers of life in the late twentieth century, a life often threatened by guns, drugs, gangs, and other non-Austenian violence, and enjoy the relative peace of Austen's depiction of the English countryside of the 1790s and 1800s.

MARRIAGE, DIVORCE, AND CUSTODY: AMERICAN LAW IN THE 1990s

In Austen's England, marriage was truly a lifetime commitment. It was extremely difficult even for a very wealthy and highly placed aristocratic man to obtain a divorce, and for the rest of the British population, it was impossible. If a couple did separate (with or without a divorce), the husband had full rights to the children automatically, since the law treated children as property, and the property of the marriage (including the children and any money that the wife earned or inherited) belonged automatically, by law, to the husband.

In the United States of the late twentieth century, despite some changes, marriage law is still based on the same British common law that existed in the late eighteenth century and the early nineteenth century. The definition of marriage remains very similar to what it was in Austen's time. The California Civil Code (1995) defines marriage as

> a personal relation arising out of a civil contract between a man and a woman, to which the consent of the parties capable of making that contract is necessary. Consent alone will not constitute marriage; it must be followed by the issuance of a license and solemnization as authorized by this code. (Crouch 1–1.1 A)

Note, however, that marriage, as defined by twentieth-century United States law, is not necessarily a lifelong contract. It is a civil contract between a man and a woman that allows them to be recognized as having a particular status under the law for as long as they both choose to have it.

The requirements a couple must meet continue to be very similar to those that a couple had to meet in Austen's time. A valid marriage in the United States at the present time requires

1. a personal relationship between one man and one woman (this requirement is under dispute at the moment with the current debate over Hawaii's passage of a law that accepts same-sex marriages);
2. the legal consent of both parties;
3. that both parties be of legal age or that the marriage be formally approved by a parent or guardian;
4. that both parties be of sound mental capacity; and
5. the fulfillment of the marriage license and solemnization requirements of the state in which the marriage takes place.

The areas in which marriage creates legal consequences likewise differ little from those areas of law affected by marriage in the early nineteenth century. When a couple marries, they still create a duty to provide necessary support for a spouse (even when separated) and for children born into the marriage, although the specific mechanisms by which that support is provided have changed over time. They still create a marital estate, although it no longer belongs exclusively to the husband. Inheritance rights are created by the marriage, establishing the surviving spouse's right to at least a portion of the deceased spouse's estate. And, of course, children born in marriage are legitimized under the law, providing for a range of privileges not automatically available to children born out of marriage.

The primary difference between marriage in Austen's time and in our own is the ease with which couples can be divorced and what results from such easy dissolution of the marriage bond. The divorce rate for first marriages in the United States is now over 55 percent; for subsequent marriages it is even higher. Therefore, regardless of couples' promising " 'til death do us part" in the vast majority of marriage ceremonies, most marriages will not be ended by the death of one of the partners, but by legal dissolution. As a result, most marriage law in the late twentieth century focuses on divorce, on the conditions necessary for the ending of a marriage and the consequences of that ending.

No longer does an individual have to petition Parliament (in the United States, Congress would be the equivalent legal body) for a divorce; no longer does it necessarily cost a fortune to get a divorce, and no longer does one have to prove heinous deeds on the part of a spouse to receive a divorce. In fact, no-fault divorce is now available in all fifty states. Divorce can still be sued for on the grounds of adultery, physical cruelty, mental cruelty, or desertion, but it can also be granted without proving (or even charging) such crimes against one's spouse. In some states, one does not even need an attorney to do the paperwork for a simple divorce (one without division of complicated assets or child custody and support to determine). Do-it-yourself divorce kits are available that a couple can use to prepare all the legal documents necessary for dissolution of the bonds of matrimony, making divorce as simple and inexpensive as possible.

There is currently a movement under way in several states to reduce the ease with which people can divorce, to return to a situation in which the marriage commitment is treated, by law, as inviolable except under the most extreme circumstances. Those involved in that movement express concern particularly for the children of divorced and divorcing parents, pointing to the large percentage of children from divorced homes who have great difficulty with school and with life. These children, say the proponents for stricter divorce laws, would greatly benefit by the state's forcing parents to take their responsibilities as spouses and parents more seriously, which, they suggest, would by necessity happen if divorce were not so easy to obtain in our society.

Perhaps one of the reasons for Austen's current popularity is that her novels focus on forming marital bonds and not on dissolving them. The world of her novels seems more peaceful and more stable than that in which we live daily. The absence of divorce and the consequences of it may contribute to that peace in a way that is very attractive to a culture suffering from so much dissolution—of marriage, of families, and of societal values.

CHOOSING A MARRIAGE PARTNER

Much of the advice given to young people in Austen's day focused on the importance of choosing an appropriate marriage partner. For women particularly, the choice of a husband could mean the difference between penury and luxury, between an emotionally comfortable life and a lifetime of emotional and physical abuse. How to determine which man would be the best husband, therefore, was a central part of the training of the young woman. How to attract, snare, and commit him to the lifelong contract of marriage demanded by eighteenth- and nineteenth-century England was the focus of the education of many women in Austen's society.

In the 1990s, Austen's readers have many more options than a single lifelong commitment to one person, even though many may prefer lifelong marriage as a lifestyle. But regardless of the number of options available, choosing a partner, whether for a lifetime commitment or for a shorter period of time, remains central to the consciousness of most females (and many males) in our culture. Magazines aimed at both the adolescent female population and at adult women often focus much of their attention on how to choose, get, keep, and/or marry a man. A sampling of article titles in popular girls' and women's magazines illustrates this point vividly:

"From the Editor: How to Succeed at Love" (Crow)

"Men: The Sixteen Most Important Things You'll Ever Learn about Them" (Frankel)

"Pickup Tricks: How to Make the First Move" (Postman)

"Ten Signs He's Crazy about You" (Ickes)

"Romance on the Rebound" (Heller)

"Quiz: Is He Getting Your Message?" (Williams)

"How to Be a Cool Girlfriend" (Maxwell)

"He Wanted a Girlfriend. I Wanted a Boyfriend. No Problem, Right?" (Braunschweiger)

"Twenty-Seven Things You Should Do Before You Say 'I Do' " (Satran)

"Men Don't Make Passes at Women Who Take Classes" (Callahan)

This list of titles demonstrates that, although a lifetime marital commitment may not be the driving force of all male/female relationships in the 1990s, romantic partnerships and the means by which to achieve and maintain them are central to the minds of many of the millions of people who purchase, read, and adhere to the value systems of the leading magazines for young women today.

The guidelines for finding and marrying the "right" man differ considerably, depending upon the article or book one reads and the family and social groups to which one belongs. Some people consider friendship and honesty to be the cornerstones of successful partnering. Others base partnership choices on the intensity of the sexual attraction. Still others think similarity of background, goals, and values is the most important consideration for successful pairing, while yet another group adheres to the old adage that "opposites attract" and therefore make the best partners.

Marriage at the end of the twentieth century is not necessarily a lifetime contract, but it continues to be viewed as one of the most important decisions people can make—even more so for women than for men. Books on the subject abound, including a few that demand particular attention due to their high profile and extreme popularity.

John Gray's *Men Are from Mars; Women Are from Venus* and Deborah Tannen's *You Just Don't Understand* head a long list of books that deal with male–female communication. These books discuss the evidence that men and women speak "different languages" even when they are using the same words. Differences in communication patterns are not always attributed to the same sources (some books focus on the biological and physiological differences of men and women, others on the different social patterning that boys and girls receive from their environment from their earliest days; yet others combine biological and environmental factors to explain the differences between male discourse and female discourse). These books teach that people who want a strong, long-lasting relationship must communicate with one another, and that to communicate effectively, they need to know both how their language will be interpreted by those of the other sex and how those of the other sex use language. Communication despite differences is the key to a good relationship, according to these authors.

Another book that has taken the best-seller charts by storm in the mid-1990s is *The Rules: Time-Tested Secrets for Capturing the Heart of Mr. Right*, by Ellen Fein and Sherrie Schneider. The title and subtitle together capture the essence of this slim volume: that any woman who behaves according to this specific set of "rules" passed down from mother to daughter through the generations can, in fact, find and marry a man who treats her as she wants to be treated. Unlike books that focus on the need for honest communication between the individuals involved in a relationship, *The Rules* demands that a woman behave according to a specific set of rules that will be likely not to communicate her full and honest feelings to her potential partner. The book jacket describes it thus:

> A simple set of dos and don'ts, THE RULES will lead you to where you want to be: in a healthy, committed relationship. Unlike today's haphazard dating customs, THE RULES recognizes certain facts of life. That men know what they want. That a man is either attracted to you—or not! That men want a challenge, not an instant or easy victory.
>
> When you follow these commonsense guidelines, you treat yourself with respect and dignity—and demand that men do likewise. . . . The goal? Marriage, in the shortest time possible, to a man you love, who loves you even more than you love him.

The Rules is a manual for girls and women of the 1990s that contains advice very similar to that found in many of the conduct books of Austen's time. Most of the rules require that a woman not make active moves, only passive ones that involve her inactivity or rejection of a man's advances. For example, a woman should not call a man, nor should she return his calls very often. She shouldn't talk to a man first, nor should she ask him to dance. She should never tell him what to do. She should hold back physically, delaying sexual contact for as long as possible. She should not open up to him too quickly, and while she should not ever be outright dishonest, she should maintain an air of mystery. One of the most important rules, one that directly relates to the conduct books of Austen's time, is that a woman should only allow herself to love a man who already loves her. In other words, just like eighteenth-century English conduct book writers John Gregory and Lady Pennington, Fein and Schneider insist that a woman must withhold her love until she is loved, that to give her heart before she knows she has been given the heart of the man in question is imprudent and irresponsible.

The popularity of *The Rules* in the mid-1990s has been phenomenal. "Rules Girls" support groups have sprung up all around the United States. Women who believe that Fein and Schneider's advice will win them the husbands of their dreams join forces to help one another stay true to "the Rules." Support for Rules Girls in the form of chat rooms and bulletin boards can even be found on the World Wide Web, indicating a large and relatively diverse audience interested in following "the Rules." Such interest in what some have labeled a return to the dark ages of male–female relationships clearly demonstrates that, at least for a large minority within the population, the more egalitarian, openly communicative, and more freely sexual relationships common to late twentieth-century single life have not, in fact, led to more happiness and fulfillment in male–female relationships than were found in previous, more restricted lifestyles.

What all these magazine articles and books have in common is a focus on developing one-on-one relationships between men and women. Marriage is not always the goal, but as the popularity of books such as *The Rules* illustrates, marriage continues to be a major goal in our society for many women, as well as for some men.

WOMEN LIVING SINGLE

In nineteenth-century England, women tended to be identified primarily in terms of their relationship to men. Wives, widows, marriageable young women, and spinsters tended to be the basic categories of identification for most women of Austen's time. Single women who were no longer considered marriageable were labeled "old maids" and "maiden aunts," with emphasis on the nonsexual and service aspects of the role.

In the twentieth century, the roles of women have changed considerably. No longer are women's identities primarily determined by their relationship to men, even though that relationship continues to be weighted much more heavily than the corresponding relationship of men to women in society's construction of individual identity. Women, both single and married, can choose employment in a wide variety of lucrative fields; they are no longer limited to service positions such as governesses, companions, and teachers in girls' academies.

Sexual mores for the single woman in the late twentieth century contrast dramatically with those of the early nineteenth century as well. While chastity continues to be valued among much of the population, a single woman who is active sexually is no longer considered "fallen"; her future is not irrevocably determined by her sexual past.

The marginal status of single women in Jane Austen's time is clear. But what about the status of the single woman in the twentieth century? In 1976 Margaret Adams published a study titled *Single Blessedness: Observations on the Single Status in Married Society.* As her subtitle indicates, single status was still considered a state outside the norm in 1976. The "society" she describes is "married"; a single person, by definition, is marginalized in such a society.

Adams discusses the role of the "maiden aunt" in some detail. This role is one in which women who were not particularly moved to marry could be useful to the larger family unit by supplying the kinds of assistance that many families must rely on social service agencies for today. For example, the maiden aunt could cook and clean for a widowed father or brother. She could act as nurse or companion to members of the extended family who were ill, incapacitated, or lonely. She could provide child care when it was needed for the children of sisters, brothers, nieces, and nephews. As Flora Young, one of the women Adams interviewed in the course of her research, put it, "There always has to be a maiden aunt in every family to be available to help out" (54). This maiden aunt phenomenon is quite familiar to anyone who studies eighteenth- and nineteenth-century England and the United States in any depth. The fact that it continues to be an accepted social role for the single woman into the latter half of the twentieth century is the surprise, considering how far most people believe women have progressed in their roles in society since Austen's time. In the mid-1960s, the role of the maiden aunt was given formal recognition when England created the National Council for the Single Woman and her Dependents. This body, according to Adams,

> has been very active in demonstrating the enormous "hidden" social services rendered by these women in taking care of family members who would otherwise become the responsibility of the public welfare services, and has campaigned vigorously for this fact to be appreciated and for the systematic assistance to be made available to lighten what can often be a seriously penalizing social burden. (54)

In her 1994 book on single women, Tuula Gordon suggests their marginal status even in her title: *Single Women: On the Margins?* Gordon interviewed many women for her sociological study of the perceptions of single women about their status in society. She discovered that most women, even those who were single voluntarily (in other words, those who had opportunities to marry eligible men whom they cared about, but chose not to do so), were ambivalent about the "old maid stereotype" to which they were often subjected. The old maid stereotype, as Gordon defines it is two-pronged: single women are "seen as old maids who could not get a man, or as modern career women who have not wanted one" (128). Such stereotypes, as Gordon explains, are "related to a perception of single women as lacking something, being incomplete, deviating from the norm and the normal" (129). Women of the late twentieth century who are single by choice resist being defined in terms of lack; whether they are sexually active or not, romantically involved or not, mothering children or not, should not, they claim, determine their social identity. The attitude of most women today, married as well as single, reflects the idea that identity should be determined by what a human being is, not by what he or she lacks.

One part of life that single women of Austen's time were expected to forego was sexual activity. Single women of the time were considered to fit neatly into one of two categories: nonsexual or fallen. Since sexual enjoyment was, at that time in history, considered to be important to men but not to women, deprivation of sexual activity was not considered to be a hardship for the spinster (except, perhaps, by some of the spinsters themselves). In the twentieth century, ideas about women's sexuality have changed significantly, as have the mores of society. While chastity continues to be cherished among many segments of society, other segments consider sexual activity a rite of passage that must be undertaken in order for the individual (male or female) to become an adult. Women no longer lose the respect of society as a whole when they engage in sexual activity outside the bonds of marriage. Such women are no longer considered to have irrevocably "fallen." Yet, a thin line often marks the boundary between what is considered reasonable sexual activity for a single woman and what makes her disreputable. A woman's reputation in regard to respectability continues to be based, to a large extent, on the degree to which she remains chaste (or at least discreet).

The relative freedom single people are permitted to exercise in regard to sexual activity in the late twentieth century has given rise to a movement sometimes referred to as "the new celibacy." This movement presents celibacy by choice, for both men and women, as a freedom to be claimed by the individual in society, a freedom to "just say no." In *The New Celibacy: Why More Men and Women Are Abstaining from Sex—and Enjoying It*, Gabrielle Brown outlines the new celibacy movement. Beginning less than a decade after the height of the "sexual revolution" in the twentieth-century United States, individuals chose to be celibate (some for life, others for particular periods of time or portions of their lives) despite the sexual freedom accepted in society at large. Brown discusses a group of people who, in 1978, spoke publicly about their decision to practice celibacy. According to Brown, they

saw it as a reaction to the "overkill" of the sexual revolution. . . . They wanted to avoid what they called The Sex Biz—to get away from it entirely. They did not want sex to be the basis for relating, with its emotional malnutrition reflected in an all-too-common experience of going to bed with people who were strangers. They concluded that sex is vastly over-rated; that throughout the nation people are no longer repressed and, therefore, that the "media

hype" of sexiness and sexual attack is no longer valid; that a sense
of a more spiritual rising consciousness is the emerging trend. (2)

When we consider the idea of celibacy, the picture that usually
comes to mind is that of the lifelong celibate, someone who, generally for religious reasons, chooses to forego sexual experience to
live a purer, more elevated spiritual life. Monks, priests, and nuns
are usually the first celibates to come to mind. Many such religious
celibates live in community situations in which the physical necessities of food and shelter are provided in common, as is social
interaction. A religious celibate community, by its very nature, acts
as a support system for the individuals within the group. Since all
members take a vow of celibacy and live in a community that is
supportive of that vow, their focus is directed toward areas other
than sexuality, generally spiritual growth and enlightenment and
service to those in need.

Secular celibacy does not function under the same conditions as
religious celibacy. First, many secular celibates do not choose lifelong celibacy. Instead, they choose to be celibate for specific periods of time and in particular situations. A young man or woman
in the contemporary celibacy movement may choose celibacy before marriage, for instance, or may choose, despite past sexual experience, to refrain from sexual activity for prolonged periods of
time. Celibacy while dating, for example, can enable the couple to
develop a strong relationship based on ideas, hopes, dreams,
goals, and so on, *before* sexual intercourse complicates the relationship. In this situation, celibacy can set the stage for a more
fulfilling and complete relationship in a subsequent marriage than
might otherwise be possible.

Secular celibacy can be chosen for other reasons as well. Young
professionals may practice celibacy while they are getting their ca-
reers off to a good start, focusing their attention on career goals
rather than being sidetracked into relationship issues. Individuals
can also choose celibacy to give themselves time, space, and energy
to devote to their spiritual, psychological, intellectual, and/or physical development.

Note that the chosen celibacy of the twentieth-century (both religious lifetime celibacy and secular celibacy of lifetime or limited
duration) is discussed without gender designators. In Austen's
time, chastity was considered to be a given for respectable single

women, but not for single men. Women were either chaste or not, "respectable" or "fallen." In the twentieth century, women and men alike are expected to be able to enjoy sexual relationships. The choice of celibacy, therefore, is available to both men and women, as is the choice of sexual activity outside marriage.

TOPICS FOR WRITTEN OR ORAL EXPLORATION

1. View one or more film or television versions of *Pride and Prejudice*. Discuss how the visual version portrayed Austen's story. Was it faithful to the events of the book? Was it faithful to the spirit of the book? Where and how did it differ from the book? How was the experience of seeing the story different from the experience of reading it? After class discussion, write an essay in which you explain which version you prefer and why.

2. Despite all the media hype about the movies and televised versions of Austen's novels in the 1980s and 1990s, no one seems to have fully described the attraction of late twentieth-century viewers and readers to Austen's works. Write an essay in which you discuss Austen mania. Discuss where you think the enthusiasm comes from and/or whether you think it is warranted.

3. Marriage in Austen's era was a lifetime commitment. In the United States in the late twentieth century, it is more often ended by divorce than by death. Hold a classroom debate on the advantages and disadvantages of each situation.

4. Compile a list of the characteristics you think would be most important in a marriage partner. Compare your list with those of your classmates and compile a list of the characteristics a majority of people in the class consider important in a marriage partner. Discuss the results.

5. Identify five magazine titles that are aimed at a female teenage and young adult audience. Collect sample issues of those magazines. Identify five magazine titles that are aimed at a male teenage and young adult audience. Collect sample issues of those magazines. Look through the tables of contents of all collected magazines and note which subjects seem to dominate in each group. Discuss what the dominance of those subjects seems to say about our culture's views of gender and equality at the present time.

6. As a class, compose a questionnaire designed to elicit people's basic ideas about relationships. Distribute the questionnaire to other students in your school or in another school (if you have Internet connections with a similar class in another town, they would be an ideal respondent group). Ask them to write their responses to your questions, revealing only their gender, not their names. When all the questionnaires have been returned, analyze the responses. Determine whether the answers met your expectations or not. Determine also what value system or systems are supported by both the questions you asked and the answers you received.

7. Have each student make a list of the single women he or she knows over thirty years of age. Then have the students discuss their perceptions of those women. Do they seem to fit into the "maiden aunt" stereotype? Are they "driven career woman" types? Or would they best be described in other terms? Discuss the place of the single woman over thirty in society. Discuss media depictions of the single woman over thirty. What, judging by both the reality students see around them and the media depictions, seems to be the attitude of our culture to single women? To what extent is it similar to that of Austen's time? To what degree does it differ?

8. In Austen's time, a woman was expected to be able to learn all that she needed to know in her own home by means of family teaching, governesses (sometimes), and books. Do you think, at the end of the twentieth century, that young women could learn all they need to know at home? If so, how? If not, why not? Be very specific about your reasoning in your response.

9. In the last decade there has been considerable discussion of the benefits and disadvantages of coeducation versus single-sex education. Which do you think benefits the majority of students most: coeducation or single-sex education? Be very specific in your reasoning.

SUGGESTED READINGS

AUSTEN MANIA

Amis, Martin. "Jane's World." *The New Yorker*, 8 Jan. 1996, 31–35.
"Austen Anew." *The New Yorker*, 21–28 Aug. 1995, 51–52.
Bellafante, Ginia. "Sick of Jane Austen Yet?" *Time*, 15 Jan. 1996, 66.
Collins, James. "Jane Reaction." *Vogue*, June 1996, 70–71.
Leonard, John. "Jane-Mania." *New York*, 15 Jan. 1996, 54–55.
Menand, Louis. "What Jane Austen Doesn't Tell Us." *The New York Review of Books*, 1 Feb. 1996, 13–15.
"Picture the Scene." *Times Educational Supplement* [London], 15 Sep. 1995, Section 2, 10–11.

MARRIAGE, DIVORCE, AND CUSTODY

Crouch, Richard E. *Family Law Checklists*. Deerfield, IL: Clark Boardman Callagher, 1995.
Perga, Mary Ann. "Marriage Is Not a Private Affair." *U.S. Catholic*, Aug. 1996, 18+.

CHOOSING A MARRIAGE PARTNER

Braunschweiger, Jennifer. "He Wanted a Girlfriend. I Wanted a Boyfriend. No Problem, Right?" *Seventeen*, Aug. 1996, 178+.

Callahan, M. "Men Don't Make Passes at Women Who Take Classes." *New York*, 10 June 1995, 16–18.

Crow, Elizabeth. "From the Editor: How to Succeed at Love." *Mademoiselle*, Jan. 1996, 77.

"Dating: How to Play the Game of Love." *Teen*, Feb. 1996, 42.

Fein, Ellen, and Sherrie Schneider. *The Rules: Time-Tested Secrets for Capturing the Heart of Mr. Right*. New York: Warner Books, 1995.

Frankel, Valerie. "Men: The Sixteen Most Important Things You'll Ever Learn about Them." *Mademoiselle*, Jan. 1996, 98–103.

Gray, John. *Men Are from Mars; Women Are from Venus. A Practical Guide for Improving Communication and Getting What You Want in Your Relationships*. New York: HarperCollins, 1992.

Heller, Anne. "Romance on the Rebound." *Mademoiselle*, June 1996, 138–41.

Ickes, Bob. "Ten Signs He's Crazy about You." *Mademoiselle*, June 1996, 134–37.

Maxwell, Jen. "How to Be a Cool Girlfriend." *Seventeen*, Dec. 1996, 74–77.

Postman, Andrew. "Pickup Tricks: How to Make the First Move." *Mademoiselle*, Jan. 1996, 119–21.

Satran, P. R. "Twenty-Seven Things You Should Do Before You Say 'I Do.' " *Glamour*, Mar. 1996, 242.

Tannen, Deborah. *You Just Don't Understand: Women and Men in Conversation*. New York: Ballantine Books, 1990.

Williams, Melissa. "Quiz: Is He Getting Your Message?" *Seventeen*, Nov. 1996, 86–88.

WOMEN LIVING SINGLE

Adams, Margaret. *Single Blessedness: Observations on the Single Status in Married Society*. New York: Basic Books, 1976.

Allen, Katherine. *Single Women/Family Ties: Life Histories of Older Women*. London: Sage, 1989.

Bequaert, Lucia H. *Single Women: Alone and Together*. Boston: Beacon Press, 1976.

Boose, Lynda E. "The Father's House and the Daughter in It: The Structures of Western Culture's Daughter-Father Relationship." In *Daughters and Fathers*. Edited by Lynda E. Boose and Betty S. Flowers. Baltimore: Johns Hopkins University Press, 1989.

Brown, Gabrielle. *The New Celibacy: Why More Men and Women Are Abstaining from Sex—and Enjoying It.* New York: McGraw-Hill, 1980.

Butler, Julie. *Gender Trouble: Feminism and the Subversion of Identity.* London: Routledge, 1990.

Chandler, Joan. *Women Without Husbands: An Exploration of the Margins of Marriage.* London: Macmillan, 1991.

Gordon, Tuula. *Single Women: On the Margins?* New York: New York University Press, 1994.

Jefferys, Sheila. *The Spinster and Her Enemies: Feminism and Sexuality, 1880–1930.* New York: Routledge and Kegan Paul, 1985.

Simon, Barbara L. *Never Married Women.* Philadelphia: Temple University Press, 1991.

Spelman, Elizabeth. *Inessential Woman: Problems of Exclusion in Feminist Thought.* London: Women's Press, 1990.

Stein, Peter, ed. *Single Life: Unmarried Adults in Social Context.* New York: St. Martin's Press, 1981.

EDUCATION FOR WOMEN IN THE 1990s

Antler, Joyce, and Sari Knopp Biklen, eds. *Changing Education: Women as Radicals and Conservators.* New York: State University of New York Press, 1990.

Belenky, Mary F., et al. *Women's Ways of Knowing: The Development of Self, Voice, and Mind.* New York: Basic Books, 1986.

Faragher, John Mack, and Florence Howe, eds. *Women and Higher Education in American History.* New York: W. W. Norton, 1988. 130–64.

Giele, Janet Zollinger. "Coeducation or Women's Education: A Comparison of Findings from Two Colleges." In *Coeducation: Past, Present, and Future.* Edited by C. Lasser. Urbana: University of Illinois Press, 1987. 91–109.

Hall, Roberta M., and Bernice Sandler. "The Classroom Climate: A Chilly One for Women?" Washington, DC: Project on the Status and Education of Women, 1982.

Martin, Jane Roland. "Redefining the Educated Person: Rethinking the Significance of Gender." *Educational Researcher* 15 (1986): 6–10.

Oates, Mary J., and Susan Williamson. "Women's Colleges and Women Achievers." *Signs* 3 (Summer 1978): 795–806.

Perun, Pamela J. *The Undergraduate Woman: Issues in Educational Equity.* Lexington, MA: Lexington Books, 1982.

Solomon, Barbara Miller. *In the Company of Educated Women: A History of Women and Higher Education in America*. New Haven: Yale University Press, 1985.

Spender, Dale. *Invisible Women*. London: Writers and Readers Publishing Cooperative Society, 1982.

Index

About the Author

DEBRA TEACHMAN is a professor and writer who divides her time between Huntington, West Virginia, where she teaches composition and literature, and Sunspot, New Mexico, where she writes and works for the National Solar Observatory/Sacramento Peak. Her research on Jane Austen began with her dissertation, "Inheritance and Expectation: The Moral Economy of Jane Austen's Fiction," for the University of California, Davis, in 1990. Since then she has presented papers on Jane Austen, Charlotte Brontë, and Edith Wharton.